JEREMIAS: MAN OF TEARS

JEREMIAS: MAN OF TEARS

By

DOM HUBERT VAN ZELLER

*They that sow in tears shall reap in joy. Casting their
seeds, they wept when going forth; but coming, they
shall return with joyfulness.*

Psalm cxxv, 5, 7.

LONDON

SANDS & CO.

(PUBLISHERS) LIMITED

15 KING STREET, COVENT GARDEN, W.C.2

AND AT 76 CAMBRIDGE STREET, GLASGOW

NIHIL OBSTAT:

      GEORGIUS CAN. SMITH, S.TH.D. PH.D.
                          Censor deputatus.

IMPRIMATUR:

      E. MORROGH BERNARD.
                  Vic. Gen.

Westmonasterii, de 17a. Martii 1941.

PRINTED IN GREAT BRITAIN BY
THE   STANHOPE   PRESS   LTD.
ROCHESTER   :   :   KENT

To GRIMA AND D'ARGY

CHRONOLOGICAL TABLE

c. 647 B.C.　Birth of Jeremias.

639 B.C.　Josias ascends throne.

627 B.C.　Call of Jeremias.　*- 20 yrs old*

621 B.C.　Finding of Deuteronomy.

609 B.C.　Mageddo.　Death of Josias.　Joachaz king.

608 B.C.　Joachim king.

c. 607 B.C.　Fall of Niniveh.

605 B.C.　Carchemesh.

597 B.C.　Death of Joachim.　Joachin king.　Sedecias king.

587 B.C.　Jeremias imprisoned.

586 B.C.　Fall of Jerusalem.

561 B.C.　Death of Nabuchodonosor.

560 B.C.　Joachin released from prison.

CONTENTS

CHAPTER		PAGE
	CHRONOLOGICAL TABLE . . .	6
	INTRODUCTION	9
I.	THE SETTING	11
II.	THE TIME BEFORE THE CALL . .	16
III.	THE CALL	23
IV.	THE PROPHET BEGINS	30
V.	HISTORICAL INTERLUDE . . .	37
VI.	THE FINDING OF THE BOOK OF DEUTER- ONOMY	41
VII.	REMAINING YEARS OF JOSIAS'S REIGN .	55
VIII.	THE DEATH OF JOSIAS	70
IX.	THE REIGNS OF JOACHAZ AND JOACHIM .	78
X.	THE TOPHETH AFFAIR	93
XI.	THE SEQUEL TO THE TOPHETH SERMON .	98
XII.	FURTHER INCIDENTS IN JOACHIM'S REIGN	107
XIII.	KING JECHONIAS	125
XIV.	INCIDENTS IN SEDECIAS'S REIGN . .	128
XV.	THE FALL OF JERUSALEM . . .	151
XVI.	AFTERMATH	157
XVII.	THE ISMAHEL SCANDAL . . .	170
XVIII.	TOWARDS EGYPT AND EXILE . .	180
XIX.	LAST PHASE	186
XX.	CONCLUSION	196
	APPENDICES	206
	BIBLIOGRAPHY	208

INTRODUCTION

I HAVE hesitated a long time before finally deciding to call Jeremias the 'man of tears'; my inclination is all in favour of calling him the 'man of singular and almost overwhelming joys.' Were I to give him this title, however, I might not be taken seriously, and to be regarded as a light-minded commentator on Holy Scripture is the last thing in the world I should want. Thus, failing the title page, it must be in the Introduction that I label the subject of this biography a man of joy.

The truth is that there are two Jeremiases. This is not to say that, from the critical and scientific point of view, there is seen to be a second mind at work in the composition of the Prophecy (in the way that there may be a 'second' Isaias or a 'second'—if not a 'third'—Zacharias), it is rather that I seem to see a single prophet who is big enough to be two very different people: he is a well of happiness besides being a fountain of tears. Fountains attract more attention, but wells are deeper. As a lamentationalist Jeremias has come down to us; it is his gift for silent laughter that has been forgotten. The gaiety of Jeremias is secret, but it is, if I am not mistaken, there. Let it not be thought that I am trying to change the traditional concept of the 'man of tears'; I am only asking people to believe that he could at times be happy, and suggesting that this has been somewhat overlooked by those who have written the best books and articles about him. Indeed, I cannot help feeling that Jeremias himself would have laughed up his camel-hair sleeve had he heard what future writers were to say about his gloom.

Having mentioned the word 'lamentation', it would be as well to say here that I do not presume to go into the question as to whether the Book of Lamentations was or was not written by Jeremias. I personally think that he did write it, and I am glad to know that in this I am following Archbishop Goodier and Fr Hugh Pope and others. The modern view is that Jeremias did not write Lamentations. In any case, the feel of the two inspired books is admitted to be so much the same that those who abide by the traditional view are well within their rights.

In conclusion I must discharge several debts of gratitude. I am grateful first of all to those whose works I have consulted and whose names appear in the Bibliography at the end. Next my thanks are due to members of my own community, some for their patience in dealing with my questions, others for helping me to wrestle with my manuscript. And lastly I want to thank the gentleman who joined me for luncheon in a confectioner's shop off Fleet Street some eighteen months ago. Not knowing his name, I am unable to send him a copy of this book. He lives in Stafford and works on the railway; that, and the fact that he came up to London on his company's ticket for a three days' holiday, is all I know about him. If my interpretation of Jeremias should ever come his way, he will be interested to see how far I have developed his thought. He will be pleased, too, I hope, to know how much I enjoyed his conversation.

What I have written I submit, as I do all else, to ecclesiastical authority, in accordance with the requirements of the Holy See.

CHAPTER I

THE SETTING

i

' JEREMIAH is one of the central figures of an exciting period which has to be reconstructed by a combined effort of criticism and imagination.' The pages which follow represent that combined effort. The words quoted are those of Dr Cheyne, the famous Biblical scholar of the nineteenth century. As far as reconstruction goes, Jeremias lends himself to the process more readily than almost any other prophet. That is the trouble. He is, if anything, too easily imagined, too easily labelled, too easily 'written up', with the result that one is inclined to miss the man's mission in the many pictures of him as a missionary. As far also as his period goes, here again we are at a disadvantage. Dr Cheyne said it was an exciting period: the trouble is that it was too exciting. Had it been a less violent epoch we could have patted it down with a few words; as it is, we shall have constantly to interrupt the prophet's story in order to provide the historical setting. That some sort of background is necessary will be seen when the text of the Prophecy comes up for examination. This book, however, will not be packed with historical allusions any more than it will be packed with critical detail. So often are biographies ruined by one or other of these excellent studies that the aim of this particular Life is to make for the central figure and not leave him.

'The words of Jeremias the son of Helcias, of
the priests that were in Anathoth in the land of
Benjamin. The word of the Lord which came to
him in the days of Josias the son of Ammon king
of Juda, in the thirteenth year of his reign. And
which came to him in the days of Joachim the son
of Josias . . . unto the end of the eleventh year of
Sedecias . . . even unto the carrying away Jerusalem
captive in the fifth month.'

The prophet, then, came of a priestly family; his
father, Helcias, was a member of the Anathoth community; the active period of Jeremias's career lay
between the years 627 and 587 B.C.[1] So much for what
the superscription tells us. We shall not be far wrong if
we make 647 as a suitable time for the prophet's birth;
he would hardly have begun to prophesy before the age
of twenty. The fact that he will be heard to call himself
a 'child' when the summons to prophesy comes to him
from the Lord is no indication that he was still a boy at
the time; it merely means that he considered himself
inexperienced in matters of the spirit.

There is reason to believe that the father, Helcias, was
the priest who discovered the Book of Deuteronomy
during Josias's reign. At all events this will be assumed
throughout the pages that follow, and since the old man
who appears in the Fourth Book of Kings is ardent in
the cause of reform we can see where Jeremias went to
for his ideas. The prophet would have been about
twenty-five years old when Deuteronomy was unearthed,

[1] 'Active' period, because, though he preached in Egypt *after*
Jerusalem's fall, his mission was primarily to prepare the Jews for
this calamity and to warn them of the dispersion.

so there is nothing unreasonable in the suggestion that the Helcias of 4 Kings was his father.

Anathoth is about three miles north of Jerusalem, in the hilly district of Benjamin. The place had been a city of the priests for generations: it is mentioned as such in the Book of Josue, and[1] we learn from 3 Kings[2] that Abiathar, the high priest in David's time, was living in retirement at Anathoth after Adonias's abortive rebellion. It was the kind of little town which would, in Our Lord's time, have had its synagogue and its regular liturgical life, but which in the seventh century B.C. boasted merely of a quasi religious community from which members were appointed to go up to Jerusalem to serve the Temple in their turn. Synagogues were not established until after the return from the captivity. It is doubtful whether there was a school at Anathoth for Jeremias to attend; he probably made the three mile journey into Jerusalem each day, but since there was almost certainly a wagon-loan of youthful students to be taken to the lectures we need not assume that he had to walk the six miles every time he attended his studies. Anathoth, now called Anata, stands some 2,500 feet above sea-level. St. Jerome says that Anathoth was a walled town of local importance. We can now leave Anathoth.

Though not of noble origin, Helcias's family seems to have belonged to the envied classes. We learn from the thirty-second chapter of the Prophecy that a certain estate came by entail into the prophet's possession, which fact, taken in conjunction with the information that he had to pay a high price for the maintenance of

---

[1] Josue xxi, 18.   [2] 3 Kings ii, 26.

his rights in this matter, suggests that the home from which Jeremias came was at least affluent.

At the time of the prophet's birth the state of religion in Juda was roughly this: Manasses, who had been on the throne for half a century, was doing all he could to break up the established order: the reforms of Ezechias were now a dead letter. Idolatry was practised openly, and there was little interest taken in the worship of the Lord. No prophet had spoken for over fifty years, and even Isaias's burning words had begun to fall cold upon the ears of the people of Juda. Born in this time of religious decline, it was for Jeremias to predict the ultimate fall. He predicted it, and suffered as a result.

If the spirit of religion was different from what it had been in the days of Isaias, so also was the spirit of the nation as a political unit. As it is natural to compare the two prophets, so it is natural to compare the two political arenas in which they wrestled. The briefest survey may suffice.

ii

Not Assyria (as it had been in Isaias's time), but Chaldea was the menace which now threatened Juda's independence. Egypt had recovered her prestige and could not be looked upon any longer as the spent force which, fifty years ago, she had shown herself to be. And if we turn from foreign politics to home affairs, we find that Juda has changed considerably under the leadership of Manasses. During the preceding reigns Isaias had fought against a transportation of his people to one or other of the Assyrian protectorates; he had encouraged above all things a hope in an ultimate consolidation at

Jerusalem. The picture fifty years later—with Manasses repainting it—shows a very different scene. The picture seventy years later—with Jeremias in the middle of his work of restoration—shows again a new grouping. The picture a hundred years later—by the time Josias's reform is under way—will be seen to change once more. That is why, throughout his career, the advice given by Jeremias to Israel was quite different from the advice given by Isaias to Israel. It is important to realise this, because from a casual reading of the two prophets we might get the impression that each represented a separate school of thought or trend of spirituality. Thus, on the one hand you have the confident Isaias urging resistance ('The Lord of hosts shall break the earthen vessel [Assyria] with terror'),[1] and on the other the melancholy Jeremias saying that it would be much better to give in ('Bend down your necks under the yoke of the king of Babylon and serve him').[2] This does not mean that the two prophets looked at things differently; it means that they looked at quite different things. Isaias could afford to resist Sennacherib in a way which Jeremias could not afford to resist Nabuchodonosor. The Chaldea of Jeremias's time was nothing like as corrupt as the Assyria of Isaias's time. Conquest at the hands of a Chaldean monarch would have meant a step up in the moral order, and Jeremias was all for making the ascent. Jeremias was every bit as Zionist as Isaias had been, but he loved his people more than he loved his Sion. Isaias was with him in this, but in the case of the earlier prophet the choice did not come up.

[1] Isaias x, 33.   [2] Jeremias xxvii, 12.

CHAPTER II

THE TIME BEFORE THE CALL

i

IF WE want to form a picture of the prophet's boy-hood we have two sources of information only: the conditions existing in Juda at the time, and the man that he became in after life.

We have seen that as regards home life Jeremias claims no pity from us on the material side. But besides creature comforts his environment included religious laxity; the boy's soul, therefore, was less at ease than his body. We cannot think of him as a prig, but we can well believe that he longed for more religion than he was getting. Religion was in his blood; his ancestors for gene-rations had been priests. And if we turn to the political conditions of Jeremias's boyhood we find that here again there was an uncongenial atmosphere surrounding him; it was the fashion to be pro-Egyptian. The trend of sympathy which prevailed in Jerusalem would have had its repercussions in the drawing-rooms, and even in the nurseries, of Anathoth. With the help of pictures and games and toys and stories, the grown-ups of Anathoth would have done their best to force their children into an Egyptian mould. This is where, in our reconstruction of the boy Jeremias, we can turn to the second source of information: we can call in the man. Knowing what we do of Jeremias's after years, we have no hesitation in claiming for the child the completest immunity from Egyptian influence.

So we imagine Jeremias as being more religious, more independent, more—if the man Jeremias is anything to go by—violent and more sensitive than the other small boys around him. In after years he was to speak of the rough treatment he had received from his friends, and though it is true that he came up against every kind of opposition later on, it was always from his enemies: no friend of his manhood—Baruch or Josias for example —ever disappointed him. May we not conclude then that the disappointments were mostly of the Anathoth period and from the people he was fond of? It is conceivably possible—though highly improbable, one feels— that Jeremias was inclined all through life to exaggerate his unpopularity; several commentators put this forward with some insistence. Which means in effect that the diminutive prophet has to be saddled with the morbid aberration known as the 'persecution complex'. If we attribute an habitual melancholy to Jeremias we make him not only a 'difficult' old man, but—which is much worse—a 'difficult' young one; the 'persecution complex' begins, I believe, at an alarmingly early age.

To think of Jeremias as building up miseries for himself is to miss the prophet's temper altogether. Sensitive, yes, perhaps too sensitive, but not subject to a neurosis. If as a boy Jeremias had trouble from his friends, we may depend upon it that the trouble was a real one. Even if Jeremias was inclined, naturally, to make mountains out of mole-hills, I submit that he was equally inclined, supernaturally, to see over the tops of them.

There is no merit in thinking of Jeremias as an exceptional creature; he was probably a perfectly ordinary little boy. If he quarrelled with his friends and was snubbed by them, at least it shows that he *had* friends, and that he liked them enough to be hurt by the way they treated him.

Mr. H. V. Morton, in one of his earlier books, gives a picture of a small boy who has fallen foul of his friends over a game of cricket in the park. 'But say what you like,' concludes the author, 'this little person walking away with dignity, the absurd dignity of the very small, was the essence of all drama: struggle, man against man, defiance; a splendid rebel . . . had I seen less clearly into his young heart I might have been one of those well-meaning idiots who go up and ask: "What is the matter, my little man? What did they do to you?" . . . Two enormous tears were rolling down his cheeks, and he was sniffing hard to keep back others. I was glad to see his feet unwavering in direction: away from compromise or surrender, going on into a solitude where there was no bat, no ball, no soft green grass.'[1] This is more the kind of young man whom we can imagine Jeremias to have resembled. If in the prophet's life we look for 'drama' (to take the words from Mr Morton's essay), then the 'essence' of it has been distilled in early youth: 'struggle, man against man, defiance; a splendid rebel'—there is the history of Jeremias in a sentence. And the 'enormous tears' of the kind just cited are the only ones which we can comfortably associate with the youthful prophet.

Oh yes, of course, the Prophecy is wet with weeping, but if the most lachrymose verses are singled out for inspection they will be seen to be the hot, indignant

[1] *The Spell of London*, p. 183.

tears of the misunderstood, or the generous tender tears
of the compassionate; never are they the slow hopeless
tears of the despairing. Resentful the prophet may have
been, but scarcely was he cynical about his boyhood.
Resentful he may have been, because an unresentful
sanctity was not yet his; though 'sanctified' while in
his mother's womb,[1] he did not start life as a saint: he
had, like everyone else, to qualify. But of cynicism there
was never any question. Cynics, besides, do not weep.
Little boys, however, do . . . particularly when they are
being ridiculed for their principles. But *then* the persecution is not a complex; rather is it a 'simplex'—the
simplest persecution in the word, the persecution of the
Cross of Christ.

ii

We are in the year 627 B.C. Two rather restless young
men, both of the same age, are waiting for something to
happen which will satisfy their longings; they have been
waiting like this for some years. So far nothing has
happened, and it looks as if nothing will.

The first of these young men is King Josias; he is just
twenty and has been on the throne for twelve years. His
father, Ammon, had reigned for one year only and was
not a success. Manasses, Ammon's father and prede-
cessor, had been still less a success. But Josias, even in
his early years of rule, had meant to break the bad tradition, and in the progress of time he was showing himself
faithful to the programme. His programme, however,
as he reviews it again now at the age of manhood, is far
more comprehensive than practical. He knows that

[1] i, 5.

only a very able administrator indeed would be able, given a strong cabinet to back him up, to carry out the social, political, and ecclesiastical reforms which are needed. He, Josias, has done his best; things have improved a great deal, and perhaps they will go on improving, but (Josias tells himself) nothing really lasting can be effected without support. The council has been asleep for fifteen years and the Temple clergy for close on fifty. What Josias wants is someone to give him a lead, someone who will tell him what are the Lord's wishes for Juda, someone who will put heart into the nation, someone who will stand uncompromisingly for the things that matter. Lord (prays Josias), I am unequal to the work; I am no genius, no super-man, no saint, I am only a rather ordinary person with good intentions. Grant me, Lord, the help I am looking for.

Then if we move from the city to the hill-side town we find the other young man, Jeremias, thinking very much the same kind of thing. He is even more depressed than Josias about the condition of religion in Juda, and for him the matter is slightly complicated by the thought of what he is going to do with himself in the future. He is not at all happy about the alternatives that offer.

We can picture Jeremias sitting at his window and looking out over a landscape which is as bleak as his own state of mind. He has spent the day in the lecture rooms of Jerusalem and is now, in that reflective hour of twilight, wondering whether such uncongenial surroundings will be his for the rest of his life: though a student, he hates the idea of studying for ever in Jerusalem. He loves the Temple liturgy, but he hates the clerical laxity.[1] On the other hand, he does not want to dis-

[1] See ii, 8, 26; v, 31; xxiii, 2.

appoint his father, Helcias. What of the other possibility—stopping at home and looking after the estate
which is to come to him in a few years' time? Presumably he could do this without offending his father,
but does he want to? The religious life at Anathoth
is as rutted as it is at Jerusalem. At Anathoth, too, he
is treated rather as a stranger, rather as a fanatic, rather
as a freak. Could he ever be happy at Anathoth? What
he wants (Jeremias tells himself) is some sort of work
which will give him scope for his zeal. Neither here nor
in the capital will he ever find the support he needs. He
knows so well what is wanted, but there is no one to
back him. Lord (prays Jeremias at his window), send
me the work which Thou willest me to do. Once fully
occupied in Thy service, I trust that these resentments
against my friends, these rebellions against the established order, these bitter judgments against mankind
at large, will pass out of my life. I see my weakness
(so we can imagine Jeremias concluding his prayer),
but I am too weak to alter it . . . because I am no saint,
no super-man, I am only a rather ordinary person with
good intentions. Grant me, Lord, the help I am looking
for.

In the palace Josias leaves his oratory and goes
upstairs to dress for dinner; in the high priest's house at
Anathoth Jeremias prepares his lamp before settling
down to an evening's work. As Josias is putting on his
purple he can see through the open window a Jerusalem
spread out as if for its sovereign's inspection. It is grey
and drab, and even the Temple—gleaming white in the
daytime—is, in this evening light, cold and lifeless. To
Jeremias, trimming his wick, the Lower Jordan Valley
looks every bit as dismal.

Let us put both men at their respective windows nine hours later, when the sun is mounting into a cloudless sky. The great Temple building is revealed to Josias in a halo of gold. 'Hallowed be God's name within His house,' is Josias's morning prayer. To Jeremias, from whom the Holy City is hidden by the shoulder of a hill, the scene presents the Dead Sea in the distance and, sloping down to the water, a stretch of dull, barren desert. But as the sun rises higher in the heavens the desert sheds its dullness, and a warm wash of colour spreads over the sea that is called Dead. Is it an earnest of the change which is to come to Jeremias's soul? Will his life soon be coloured and warmed by the light of God's love?

Jeremias, still praying that the surface of his soul may lose its bitterness and chill, goes down towards the southern gate of Anathoth and out on to the road that leads to Juda's capital.

CHAPTER III

THE CALL

i

SO WE have two would-be servants of God unable, apparently, to give full service. And then—

> 'The word of the Lord came to me saying: before I formed thee in the womb of thy mother I knew thee; and before thou camest forth I sanctified thee and made thee a prophet unto the nations. And I [Jeremias] said: Ah, ah, ah, Lord God; behold, I cannot speak: for I am a child.'

Not even Isaias was favoured quite to this extent; few are able to trace back their vocations to the time before their birth. Apart from Our Lord, the only other instances which occur in Scripture are the cases of Samson in the Old Testament and John the Baptist in the New. As a rule the grace for doing a special work for God is given to the soul when the occasion for doing it arises.

Jeremias's first reactions to the summons were, as in the similar case of Isaias, those of shrinking. All his life he had wanted to do something big for God, but when it came to the point he found himself drawing back. Perhaps it is that the nobler the soul the more it is inclined to see its own inadequacy. Certain it is that the nobler the soul the more will the powers of evil attempt to block the work it is being called upon to do.

We can find many examples of this dread on the part of God's elect: Moses, Amos, Ezechiel, and a number more. Where there is less singlemindedness there is less diffidence, and where reformers of the Jehu pattern simply put their heads down and go blindly at it, reformers of a more spiritual quality tremble at the reponsibility of their consent.

As Moses had done before him, Jeremias told the Lord that when he was excited he could not get his words out properly . . . ah, ah, ah, see, I cannot even speak, and You want me to be a prophet.[1] How can I be a messenger 'unto the nations'? I've had no experience; I'm far too young; oratory has never appealed to me; it's all a mistake; I'm quite the wrong man for the work.

> 'And the Lord said to me: Say not, I am a child.[2]
> For thou shalt go to all that I shall send thee, and
> whatsoever I shall command thee thou shalt speak.
> Be not afraid at their presence, for I am with thee
> to deliver thee.'

Jeremias's youthfulness, then, will not be taken as an excuse. With Samuel, David and Saul as precedents, Jeremias might have guessed that youth was no barrier to the work of God. It is curious to note that though the plea of being under age is the only one put forward by Jeremias, the Lord, on the other hand, takes up the possibility of his being 'afraid'. 'Be not *afraid* of your future hearers': it does not take long before the real motives of our refusals are dragged out into the light. It

---

[1] Exodus iv, 10.

[2] For proof that the word 'child' can be applied to a man of twenty it is worth while noting that the same noun is used in Exodus xxxiii, 11, for Josue, the son of Nun, who was well in the forties at the time.

is no good telling God that we are either too young or too old, or that we have not the necessary qualifications, or that we would be of much more use to Him somewhere else, when really we refuse because we are afraid.

The next verse seems to suggest that the Lord saw another excuse hovering on the lips of His servant, and so took immediate action:

> 'And the Lord put forth His hand and touched my mouth; and the Lord said to me: Behold, I have given My words in thy mouth; lo, I have set thee this day over nations and over kingdoms, to root up and to pull down, to waste and to destroy, to build and to plant.'

This is where Jeremias's experience, from being an audition only, assumes the added character of the vision. The sight of the Lord's outstretched hand, together with the symbolical act which followed, can have had but one meaning to the mind of Jeremias. Any young student of that time would have been familiar with the account of Isaias's initiation, and Jeremias would have grasped the implication at once. In his case the significance of the Lord's action was, if anything, clearer than the symbolism of Isaias's burning coal. Where the earlier prophet had complained of unclean lips and had had them cleansed, Jeremias, on the other hand, was granted positively and spontaneously the gift of prophecy. And so, whether he liked it or not, Jeremias would henceforth have to spend himself in rooting up and pulling down, in building and in planting; and the Lord would be at his side to give him strength. But note this, that not solely in pulling down and root-

ing up lay the prophet's mission: he must sow the seed
for the harvest of promise.

ii

Here follows the second part of the prophet's mystical
experience. The Lord showed Jeremias an almond tree
and a boiling cauldron. Our version has, instead of the
almond tree, a 'rod watching', but since authorities seem
to be agreed on the same implication, the differences of
form need not bother us. The almond is the first tree
to blossom, and so, heralding the approach of spring,
is the emblem of wakefulness.[1] Jeremias was to understand that the Lord was about to rouse Himself and that
Juda's winter was at an end. The meaning of the
cauldron ('the face thereof to the north') is not altogether
clear; probably it was intended to stand for Juda, whose
people should be wasted away by the flames of an enemy
and whose main danger would be seen to approach from
the north. This important chapter closes with the following three verses:

> 'Thou therefore gird up thy loins and arise, and
> speak to them all that I command thee. Be not
> afraid at their presence: for I will make thee not to

[1] See Thomson, *The Land and The Book*, p. 318. This work is a
mine of odd bits of information; it numbers 700 pages and contains
many rather surprising illustrations ('The Tomb of Jonas' is one,
and 'Mode of Playing The "Ood" ' is another). The book was pub-
lished in the seventies and has been reprinted a number of times;
it is well worth looking through, but hardly deserves a cover-to-
cover study. The main merit of the work lies in the painstaking way
in which the author has gone about his purpose. If we want a sample
of nineteenth century travel writing, *The Land and the Book* is
typical of its kind; *as* typical as Mr Beverley Nichols is typical of
the twentieth century. Mr Nichols covers the same kind of ground
as Dr Thomson in *No Place Like Home*.

fear their countenance. For behold I have made thee this day a fortified city and a pillar of iron and a wall of brass, over all the land, to the kings of Juda and the princes thereof, and to the priests and to the people of the land. And they shall fight against thee and shall not prevail: for I am with thee, saith the Lord.'

Again the injunction not to fear. Jeremias was evidently still showing signs of being frightened. But he need not have worried; he would be perfectly safe under the care of the Lord: impregnable as a fortress, immovable as a tower of iron, resonant as a brazen wall. The mention of Juda's 'kings'—in the plural— suggests a warning that the prophet's labours were to be spread over a considerable period of time; during no less than five successive reigns was Jeremias to exercise his office. In addition to the kings he would have to correct 'princes', 'priests', and 'people', which meant that his own father would come in for his rebukes —to say nothing of his uncles, cousins, fellow students and friends.[1] We are hardly surprised that Jeremias trembled at the prospect; the thought that his scarcely broken voice would soon be raised in the court, in the Temple, in the 'stately home' and in the house of his father, was enough to stagger a less sensitive youth than Jeremias.

It is perhaps a pardonable digression to compare the grace which we have just seen granted to the prophet with a similar favour received by a very much later servant of God, Denis the Carthusian. In A.D. 1451,

[1] That the prophet had much to endure from his brethren, whether before or after he reproved them, is shown by some bitter retrospections. See ix, 2-5; xii, 6-7; xx, 10.

on the Feast of the Purification, Denis was commissioned by God to do for the Church much what Jeremias 2,000 years before had been told to do for Juda. Rome of the fifteenth century A.D. was crying as loud for correction as Jerusalem of the seventh B.C. But the parallel which we want here to consider is more between the two men than between the times in which they worked.

Not only was the monk, as was the prophet, required to wrestle with kings, princes, church dignitaries and lay people, but he seems to have felt the same reluctance as Jeremias felt in undertaking the work. There is in the two men a common diffidence blended with a common resolve. They show the same love for a sinful people and—as we shall see when we come to know more of the prophet Jeremias—the same sense of oppression at the sight of rejected love. Denis more than any subsequent reformer (so it seems to me) echoes the prophet's groan of personal failure. Anyone reading the Carthusian's letters[1] cannot fail to be struck by the likeness which they bear to some of the non-narrative portions of Jeremias's Prophecy. Perhaps the similarity is not accidental: Denis, before he turned his attention to Church reform, wrote a number of homilies on the prophet's work. But the likeness is not confined to this. To each man was granted what seems to have been the same kind of mystical revelation or rapture in which the plans of God were unfolded and which made all the difference to their lives. Where the monk used the written word, the prophet used the spoken word: both men demanded the same unqualified change of heart. Denis looked for remedy to a Council,

[1] *Opera Minora*, which begin with the thirty-seventh volume of his complete works.

Jeremias to a Captivity. In the end, after years of prayer and dwindling hope, Denis looked only to the personal sanctification of its members for the final recovery of the Church. In the end Jeremias did the same. Both were visionaries, both were idealists. Both admitted defeat, yet each succeeded in his mission . . . which was to preach the way of penance, and not, apparently, to achieve results. When they came to die the two men were broken with age and disappointment; but they seem to have acquired one thing with declining years—serenity. Having fought like tigers all their lives for the things which they judged to be of God, they shared in the end the same glorious peace. Not the peace of victory, but the peace of submission: submission to the victory of God's Will.

CHAPTER IV

THE PROPHET BEGINS

i

THIS is the place to say that the Prophecy is not in chronological order. A number of editors have tried their hands at recasting the prophet's words at one time and another, with the result that it is no easy matter to follow the sequence of the prophecies as actually delivered.[1] Even the patient Origen seems to have been much exercised in mind as to how some of the transpositions can have come about. In this book I am presuming to pass over all discussions as to when this or that sermon was preached, and will endeavour—after consulting the standard authorities—to dovetail the prophetical and narrative portions of the Prophecy into a more or less readable form. A tentative synopsis is printed at the end.

Though it is more than probable that the chapter which follows the account of the call does not represent the prophet's first sermon, it can come up here for examination as being a true summary of Jeremias's thought in the first years of his apostolate. Critics are ready to admit that the second chapter is almost certainly the prophet's revised version—condensed and amended years later—of addresses he had delivered at the beginning. Throughout Jeremias's work, as a fact,

[1] See Dr Peel's article 'Jeremiah: The Book in Outline,' in *The Story of the Bible*, p. 695.

there is evidence of a tendency to look back and sum up. The whole of his Prophecy might be described as a flood of tears that has petrified at intervals. Here however the writer is looking forward as well as looking back: he is giving us the sum of the prophecies to come.[1]

The chapter is a long one; it tells us in greater detail what is already gathered in a general way from the Books of Kings and Paralipomenon. We learn, for example, that the precise evils of which the clergy were guilty at this time were idolatry and ignorance of theology. How far Jeremias can be said to have been successful in changing this state of affairs it is difficult to say: there were hardly any Temple clergy left by the time Jeremias had ceased to preach. The fall of Jerusalem and the subsequent dispersion scattered the wayward members of Jerusalem's priesthood. In the chapter before us we see Jeremias declaring his open hostility. We are not surprised when we hear that his family and his companions resented his attitude. If up till now he had been looked upon with no very kindly eye, he was, after his first sermon or two, looked upon with detestation.

For some thirty verses of the text Jeremias is as vitriolic as one could wish, and then there comes a passage which, though still bitter, is able to provide us with some highly gratifying indications. In the gruff and rather forbidding ascetic which Jeremias is commonly made out to be, it is pleasing to note his choice

---

[1] That this chapter is an important one is seen from the range of subject matter; the following themes are enlarged upon:

(a) Israel's ingratitude in the face of the Lord's repeated advances.

(b) The effect of this upon the nation; the necessary remedy.

(c) The evil of idolatry, and the folly (apart from the wickedness) of not trusting in God alone.

(d) To have denied the sin is not to have excused it; punishment must follow the apostasy of the nation.

of simile. 'Will a virgin forget her ornament,' he cries, 'or a bride her waist-band?' No, of course she won't, is the answer, yet Juda has forgotten the gifts of God. The impossible *has* happened: Jehovah *has* been discarded—as no longer fashionable: new gods have taken His place. The bride has sold her wedding dress. Evidently Jeremias has not held himself so far aloof from ordinary life as not to notice the attention which his young cousins have given to their ear-rings and necklaces and trousseaux. On the whole, however, the Prophecy is lacking in ornament of the kind just quoted. The work corresponds to the popular conception of the writer. Here in the early part of the Prophecy the style is considerably more uniform than what is met with towards the end. With the later flashes of autobiography there is noticeable a tone of poignant and personal grief. The colour of the whole is thereby deepened as the work proceeds, at the expense, it would seem, of the original unity.

To conclude the survey of this first section of prophecy it is interesting to note the difference between the two wordings of verse 36 according to the Catholic and Protestant texts. Where the Revised Version has: 'Why gaddest thou about so much to change thy way?' the Vulgate reads: 'How exceeding base art thou become, going the same ways over again!' This is surely one of the places where we are allowed the happier rendering. What a wealth of reproach lies behind the latter text— where we have the suggestion of repeated and repeated and repeated infidelity on Juda's part. And how tame in comparison is the rebuke 'Thou gaddest about.' The one has all the sorrow of a man who has married an unworthy woman, the other has all the petulance of a guardian who is inclined to nag. Whatever it is in the Hebrew, let us congratulate ourselves on the English. 'How exceeding base art thou become, going the same ways over again'. The words are charged with meaning.

ii

Then if we ask *what* ways did the Jews go over again, we have the answer on almost every page of the Chosen People's history. Often though they have been punished for so doing, the Jews have again and again gone after other loves. If it was not an idol it was a nation, if it was not an 'unbelieving custom' it was a system of government, a style of architecture, a matrimonial liberty borrowed from the 'peoples round about'. 'And thou shalt be ashamed of Egypt, even as thou wast ashamed of Assyria,' concludes Jeremias; and what bitter reflexion these words invite! You will tire of this lover as you have tired of others. Did not Isaias prove to you what harm must inevitably follow if once you give in to this fickleness of your nature? *Then* it happened to be Assyria that was the attraction, now it happens to be Egypt. Well, you shall see, O Israel, what good it does you to trust in any arm save God's.

As with nations so with individuals: each has his own weakness to which he is particularly inclined. A man's temperament will shadow him all his life, and the sooner he recognises this the better. We have it all in Our Lord's parable of the wheat and the cockle. In all of us the cockle is *there*, and will be until the time of harvest; it merely remains for us so to arrange matters that it is not given precedence over the wheat. We cannot

entirely oversow the cockle, because man may not force
an artificial solution to a problem which—to him—is
fundamental. We cannot say: 'There is a flaw in my
composition; therefore I will change myself.' We must
say: 'There is a flaw in my composition; therefore I
shall always be the same.' But of course we must not
settle down to allowing free play to our weakness: we
must think out a way of coping with it. The parable, if
read wrongly, is defeatist; if read rightly, it teaches us
that we must be prepared to meet the same temptation
again and again, and this not because history has a way
of repeating itself, but because weakness has a way of
re-asserting itself. Human nature makes its own history
—out of its own particular weaknesses and strengths.
So of course history will repeat itself. But far from
predestinating a people—still less a soul—to an inevitable mode of action, this principle should dispose a
people—or a soul—towards meeting the now familiar
occasions of failure. We keep covered those spots which
past experience has shown us to be tender. The cockle,
after all, does not stifle the wheat unless the wheat is
prepared to be stifled. The wheat can 'take it': it is
built to take it.[1] The fault with Israel, as Jeremias
was at pains to point out, lay as much in denying its sin
as in committing it. 'Behold, saith the Lord, I will
contend with thee in judgement because thou hast said:

[1] In the ordinary way the terminology of the world should be
avoided when commenting on the things of the spirit. In this case,
however, there seems justification for the liberty. The shade of
meaning conveyed by the term 'to take it' is precisely that which
St John expresses in the first chapter of his Gospel. 'The light
shineth in the darkness and the darkness did not *comprehend it*.'
It is better in the Greek: αὐτὸ οὐ κατελαβεν—did not 'take it'.
Thus it is not strictly a use of slang to say that the wheat was made
capable of 'taking' the cockle: it is going back to St. John's verb,
κατάλαμβάνω—to lay hold of, to superimpose itself, to occupy.

I have not sinned.' Since Israel would not look at the cockle, the Lord would not look at the wheat.

iii

For two reasons we can safely assume that Jeremias left Anathoth not long after receiving the call to prophesy. And for the same reasons we may judge that from then onwards he made Jerusalem his home, leaving it only—as we shall see when the Book of the Law has been unearthed—to preach the word in the cities and villages round about. The reasons are these: first, if it was his mission to appeal in person to the heart of Juda, he would have wanted to be on the spot in the capital itself; and second, if he found himself constantly having to attack his own relations, he would hardly have wanted to go on living with them. At least in Jerusalem he would be free of his family, and they would be free of him. 'Oh, that I had a lodging place for wayfaring men . . . that I might leave my people and go from them. For they are adulterers, an assembly of treacherous men.' He evidently found his lodging place, because we hear him saying (from within the walls of the Holy City): 'I have forsaken my house, I have left my inheritance; my inheritance is become to me as a lion in the wood: it hath cried out against me, therefore have I hated it.' One ventures to think that Jeremias probably 'cried out' first. The verse conjures up, one feels, a rather ugly scene. If, furthermore, the prophet really means what he says about the lion and the wood, it looks as if he never went back again to Anathoth; let us hope that some of his friends—the

less leonine of the sylvan community—braved Jeremias's
wrath occasionally, and came to see him in Jerusalem.
Certainly Helcias, his zealous father, retained the prophet's confidence. But this is a page in the biography
upon which it does not do to dwell; the comfort is that
there is little enough on it to read.[1]

[1] The passage in chapter xx where Jeremias complains that his
'familiars' have turned against him refers to his fellow workers in
Jerusalem and not to his associates of the Anathoth period.

CHAPTER V

HISTORICAL INTERLUDE

TO SUMMARISE the march of events in Juda up
to date: Five years before Jeremias received his
call, Josias had begun to take steps against idolatry;[1] in
the twelfth year of his reign he renewed his efforts along
the same lines;[2] in the year following, with the evidence
of Jeremias's first public prophecies before him, he was
able to see that the movement was being crowned with
a measure of success.[3] We must now look outside the
territory of Juda, and note how far the politics of other
peoples were influencing the history of the Jews. We
shall then be able to see that, great as these external
influences were, perhaps even more important and far-
reaching in its effects was the homely little episode of a
certain priest turning up a forgotten manuscript amid
the dust and lumber of his sacristy.

The decay of Assyria had, as has already been suggested, become apparent. Niniveh's conquests, which
had opened like a fan over Palestine, had come to an
end. The famous Assyrian armies, which had scarcely
known the meaning of home life, were now within their
own borders, keeping out the Medes and Persians. With
the concentrating of forces at home, the colonies of

---

[1] 2 Paralipomenon xxxiv, 3.   [2] 4 Kings xxiii.

[3] Josias certainly needed this encouragement, because there were
still five years to wait before the event was to take place which would
give the first really effective impetus to the forces of reform. This
event was the finding of the Book of the Law.

Assyria were gradually slipping from her grasp: Egypt under Pharaoh Necho rebelled; Babylon under Nabopolassar followed suit. But there was another nation in the field. Not only could Juda watch Egypt gathering strength in the south and Babylon gathering strength in the east, but it could also note the ominous approach of Scythia from the north. It all looked as if Juda would soon be caught up in the toils of war. The Jewish politicians were alive to this danger, and so did their best, by fanning the flame of pro-Egyptian feeling, to play off one power against another. It was this which so infuriated Jeremias. But to the infuriated prophet Juda replied that even if Egypt should prove as fickle a friend as he feared, the Scythians would at least be kept at arm's length by the news of the alliance.

A better source of information on the Scythian question than either Jeremias or the Books of Kings is the prophet Sophonias. Jeremias's reticence may perhaps be accounted for by the suggestion that when, years later, he came to write out the sermons he had preached at this period his mind was still so full of the greater menace—the growth of Babylon's power—that he thought Scythia hardly worth mentioning. And as a fact, even Sophonias does not mention them by name. All the authorities are agreed, however, that the armies he mentions as having triumphed over the Philistines, the Moabites, the Ammonites and the Assyrians, can only have been those of the Scythians.[1] Sophonias tells how 'Gaza shall be destroyed; Ascalon shall be as a desert; Azotus, shall be cast out at noonday, and Accaron

---

[1] A memorial to the activities of this warlike people is to be found in the name of a little town in Galilee, Scythopolis, where the population remained non-Jewish at least until the time of the historian Josephus.

shall be rooted up.'[1] We know from other sources that these names were, as it turned out, among Scythia's defeated enemies.[2] Mesopotamia, from being the envied kitchen-garden of that part of the world, was reduced to the poverty of a desert waste, and the sea-board, from Mount Carmel in the north to Gaza in the south, was overrun.

What with Jeremias crying out against Egypt and Sophonias crying out against Scythia, it must have been no very comforting experience to listen to the prophets in those days of Jerusalem's uncertainty. The fact that these two servants of God were working in Juda at much the same time introduces a fertile source of speculation—the speculation that in all probability they were friends. There is certainly a likeness between the writings of the two men (which suggests that they knew each other), though the question as to who borrowed from whom is still being discussed by the experts. Sophonias was the senior in point of age, and one likes to think that Jeremias went to him for guidance in matters spiritual. Briefly, the history of Sophonias is as follows: born of royal stock (he was the great-great-grandson of king Ezechias, the contemporary of Isaias), he prophesied for a short time during the reign of Josias, whom he probably predeceased. From the knowledge he shows of Jerusalem it is assumed that he spent his life in the capital; and, from various mannerisms and references, it is further assumed that he mixed freely with the life of the court. Sophonias is commemorated in the Roman Martyrology on December 3rd, the day on which the Church keeps the feast of St. Francis Xavier. Two more different types of sanctity it would be difficult to imagine.

[1] Sophonias ii, 4, 5.   [2] Ezechiel xxxiii, 9-15.

Jeremias could have learned much from the older prophet, who seems to have been able to live among the things of this world without prejudice to those of the next. One likes to think that the courtier-saint softened down some of the sharper edges on Jeremias's soul. In the younger man we see a strange mixture of qualities: he is bitter against his family and diffident about his powers. Is it not possible that Sophonias (who himself could say some hard things about his own relatives, royal though they were)[1] tamed the fierceness by giving an example of leniency, and cured the diffidence by giving to Jeremias something of his own confidence in God? We like to think of Sophonias running his eye over the neophyte's sermon notes . . . 'Too savage, my dear Jeremias, too savage' . . . until a phrase is hit upon which will tell of the love which, in different ways, the two men bear for the wayward, sinful, thankless, yet infinitely-worth-while-saving sons of Juda.

[1] Sophonias i, 8; iii, 3.

CHAPTER VI

THE FINDING OF THE BOOK OF DEUTERONOMY

i

MATERIAL for this chapter is drawn from 4 Kings and 2 Paralipomenon; the Prophecy will not be of much use to us here, because Jeremias seems to have had no desire to chronicle events until after Josias's death. All that he has given us hitherto has been either autobiography or strict prophecy: the history we have had to piece together from other sources.

This is the account from 4 Kings xxii, and though the passage is a long one it is clearly necessary to print it in full; it can be broken up, however, at intervals.

'In the eighteenth year of king Josias, the king sent Saphan the scribe to the Temple of the Lord, saying to him: Go to Helcias the high priest, that the money may be put together which is brought into the Temple of the Lord, which the doorkeepers have gathered of the people.' (Here follow some instructions as to how these sums were to be spent; the text goes on:) 'And Helcias the high priest said to Saphan the scribe: I have found the Book of The Law in the house of the Lord. And Helcias gave the Book to Saphan, and he read it.'

It is easy to reconstruct the scene; in fact it is rather difficult not to. We see Saphan coming into one of the

Temple's ante-chambers in search of his friend Helcias.
The whole building is under repairs, and the halls and
galleries echo to the sound of hammering. Helcias has
been tidying up, and is found seated on the edge of an
open chest with a sheaf of worm-eaten parchments in
his lap. Saphan's message from Josias is delivered, but
not listened to. Helcias says quite simply and without
comment: 'I have found Deuteronomy'.[1] As a matter
of fact, of course, no explanation was needed: the scribe
knew as well as the priest what would be the effect of
such a discovery. Both men had only been waiting for
some such chance as this to further their hopes for Juda's
betterment.

> 'And Helcias gave the Book to Saphan, and he
> read it.'

An hour later the two men were still in the same room;
Saphan had read the volume from cover to cover. Yes,
Helcias was undoubtedly right: it *was* the Book of the
Law. What was the next move? Ought they to show it
to Sophonias the court prophet?—or would the shock
of the thing hasten the old gentleman's decline? Ought
Jeremias, the young messenger of Jehovah, to be
approached?—or would everyone say afterwards that
the Helcias family had shown a too proprietary attitude towards the affair? No, the best thing to do was to
see the king about it straight away.

> 'And Saphan the scribe came to the king and
> brought him word concerning that which he had

---

[1] I am taking it for granted that the Book of the Law *was* Deuteronomy. Commentators are agreed that if the newly-discovered text
was not identical with that which has come down to us under the
name of Deuteronomy, it was at least the same in substance.

commanded, saying: Thy servants have gathered
together the money which was found in the Temple
of the Lord, and they have given it to be distri-
buted to the workmen . . . and Saphan the scribe
told the king saying: Helcias the priest hath delivered to me a book.'

There was evidently not a great deal of deliberation;
the two men wrapped up the tattered volume and left
the Temple for the palace. We can see them treading
delicately over the débris and between the great blocks
of newly-quarried masonry. The day is almost over
and the workmen are gathering up their tools and
shaking the stone-dust from their clothes. Scaffold
poles and temporary platforms—seen in the gloom of
dusk—give to the Temple a new architectural character
. . . there is the smell of damp plaster . . . ropes and
buckets and planks lie in a rich profusion on the tiles
of the holy place[1] . . . outside in the street the lamps
are being lit and the children are being sent to bed.

Saphan did not take Helcias with him into the king's
presence; nor did he immediately break the news of his
friend's discovery. Instead, with true ministerial discretion, he first dispatched the business which he had
been told earlier on in the day to carry out. When the
field was clear for his disclosure, 'Helcias,' he announced,
'hath delivered to me a book.' And he produced it from
the folds of his *talith*.

[1] The work of restoration in the Temple was part of the king's
general plan to awaken a sense of religion in his people. It was two
hundred and fifty years since the Temple had last been renovated,
so it doubtless needed the attention. The previous occasion was
under Joas (4 Kings, xii, 7-14); Joiada (who more or less ran the
kingdom as well as the Temple during his sovereign's minority)
was the high priest of the period.

> 'And when Saphan had read it before the king,
> and when the king had heard all the words of the
> law of the Lord, he rent his garments.'

So for the second time that afternoon Saphan read
right through Deuteronomy. This time it was out loud
and to a listener who was as excited as himself. There
was still something of the schoolboy in Josias (after all,
he was only just twenty-one), and in any case the idea
of a buried treasure come to light is one which appeals
to everybody. Then as Saphan turned the last page
and was clearing his throat for the dramatic eulogium of
Moses, Josias got up from his throne and 'rent his garments'. We can think of several reasons why the king
did this. He saw (this is what the commentators tell us)
how far his people had been from the true observance
of the law. He also saw how far he himself was from the
standard required of God's elect, and how unequal he
was to enforce all that he had just heard. He saw and
dreaded the punishment which would have to come as a
sequel to the neglect. There are a number of reasons
why Josias should have rent his clothes. May we suggest
a further one? He rent his garments because he was a
rather violent young man, and there was nothing much
else he could, on the spur of the moment, do. A highly-
strung person who has been listening for over an hour
to what his wildest dreams have never painted for him
will naturally want to express himself somewhat for-
cibly. The occasion calls for a demonstration of some
sort, and where in another age a man—say a medieval
prince—would give a dinner or free a serf or kill a
Saracen, Josias in the seventh century B.C. judges that
under the circumstances the gesture most suitable to the
occasion is the ritual act of rending the outer garment.

'And he [Josias] commanded Helcias the priest and Ahicam the son of Saphan the scribe, and Asaia the king's servant, saying: Go and consult the Lord for me and for my people and for all Juda concernthe words of this book which is found; for the great wrath of the Lord is kindled against us because our fathers have not hearkened to the words of this book.'

Josias realised at once that this discovery placed in his hands the handle which might turn on the engines of reform, and knew well enough at the same time that for the reform to be successful it would need to be furthered by the spiritual and political leaders in the kingdom. So he chose a band of laymen and priests who could be relied upon and sent them off to 'consult the Lord'. Not to consult each other, but to consult Jehovah. And for this consultation a recognised messenger of God was necessary.

'So Helcias the priest, and Ahicam, and Achobor, and Saphan, went to Holda the prophetess the wife of Sellum the son of Thecua, the son of Araas keeper of the wardrobe, who dwelt in Jerusalem in the Second:[1] and they spoke to her.'

Allowing that Sophonias was dead by this time we would have thought that if Josias wanted to know the will of the Lord he would have consulted the prophet Jeremias. And yet we find that the person chosen to reveal God's purpose in the matter was someone we have never heard of before, and that a woman. The

[1] The 'Second' (in the Hebrew, 'Mishneh') is sometimes translated by 'the college'. In Professor Lumby's Commentary we read that the Second was 'probably some additional suburban portion of the city'.

text-books find a number of facts which can account for the passing over of Jeremias, but they seem to miss the most important fact of all—which is that Josias had no need to consult anybody about the will of God, because the will of God was perfectly clear already. This being so, and because—as already suggested—an *imprimatur* from some reputed authority would be of value to the movement, once it was started, better *any* oracle be chosen other than one of his own circle. So long, that is, as the prophet was manifestly of God—and not likely to falsify the Word—it was obviously more politic to hit upon a name that was not connected with reform. Josias's friends were marked men. The king was so certain that the whole thing was of God that he could safely leave it in a stranger's hands—in a lady's in fact.

A word on the prophetess Holda. Apart from Miriam, the sister of Moses, Holda is the only woman in the Bible for whom is claimed the gift of prophecy; Isaias's wife is called a 'prophetess', but here it is simply a courtesy title—as it is in the case of Anna the daughter of Phanuel, mentioned in St. Luke's Gospel. According to the Septuagint version, Holda was Sellum's mother, μήτηρ, not his wife. I am told that whereas most people can easily picture the dancing Miriam, few have a mental image of the lady Holda. This is surprising, because I find I have to use real self-restraint in order *not* to picture her. A file of at least a dozen prophetesses appear before me the moment I see her name upon the page. There is the youthful and wide-eyed ecstatic; there is the aged recluse; there is the thin-lipped spouse (or mother) of the overshadowed Sellum; there is the ample matron, kindly and serene, who is always ready to play strange games with Sellum's offspring; there is the capable leader of every social work connected with the 'Second in Jerusalem.' ...

We need not examine the prophetess's reply to the king's embassy, because it was exactly what we would have expected it to be. It was certainly what the king expected it to be. Holda said that Deuteronomy was clearly the word of God and that it had to be obeyed. She said, further, that certain evils would come upon Juda for her idolatry, but that as Josias had not been to blame for the people's sin he need not fear the people's punishment. Holda's message takes up the last six verses of the chapter and closes the first part of the episode. We hear no more of Holda.

ii

The immediate sequel to the finding of Deuteronomy is, though not strictly germane to the course of Jeremias's career, so important in the consideration of seventh century Juda (*and* so satisfactory from the narrative point of view) that it cannot well be left out. The account is from the same source as before.

> 'And he [the king] sent, and all the ancients of Juda and Jerusalem were assembled before him. And the king went up to the Temple of the Lord and all the inhabitants of Jerusalem with him, the priests and the prophets and all the people both little and great. And in the hearing of them all he read the words of the book of the covenant which was found in the house of the Lord. And the king stood upon the step and made a covenant with the Lord to walk after Him and to keep His command-

ments and His testimonies and His ceremonies, with all their heart and soul . . . and the people agreed to the covenant.' (Here follow twenty verses describing the measures taken to enforce the covenant; the passage concludes:) 'Moreover, the diviners by spirits, and soothsayers and the figures of idols and uncleannesses and the abominations that had been in the land of Juda and Jerusalem Josias took away, that he might perform the works of the Law that were written in the book which Helcias the priest had found in the Temple of the Lord.'

There seems to have been first a council at which the 'ancients' alone were assembled, and then this general meeting in the Temple of 'all the people both little and great'. How was 'all Juda' represented? Did the heads of families attend in the main body of the building (while their children and grandchildren waited, expectant and envious, in one or other of the outer courts), or were men alone admitted, the rest having to content themselves with seats in the open air? We do not know, but in any case there must have been little room to spare. 'Priests, prophets, and all the people both little and great'; Jeremias was there, then, and the lady Holda. Some of Jeremias's Anathoth connexions would also have been present. One wonders if Jeremias bowed to them as he took his place, and whether they discussed him as they went back to Anathoth that evening. Let us hope that the 'lions' of Anathoth, once away from the 'wood', were gracious enough to hide their malice under the silken cloak of civility.

'In the hearing of them all Josias read all the words of the Book of the Covenant.''

We can stage for ourselves this memorable scene. The waiting crowd would, even in the subdued light of the Temple interior, have been a riot of colour. We can hear the hushed voices of many men asking each other the reason for the summons, we can see the billowing of incense, the flickering of numberless candles, the play of light and shade on the newly-restored walls. Then a ripple runs along the sea of heads and, as the men at arms march towards the raised throne, silence settles upon the audience. Following the guard come various civic dignitaries, and then the nobles; after these again the priests and the prophetical school; then the king's personal suite, and last of all Josias. At a given signal, and when the king has taken his place, everyone sits down. The ceremony has opened.

We are distinctly told that Josias read the book first, then made the covenant, and *then* obtained the consent of the people. We would have expected the consent to come before the covenant. As a fact, what probably happened was this: Josias, having read the text of Deuteronomy, publicly and with his face towards the altar, proclaimed his intention of abiding by it *in toto* as far as he was concerned (this is the 'covenant'); he then turned round and invited his people to do the same. 'And the people agreed to the covenant.'

A number of half idle questions suggest themselves. Did Josias really read right through Deuteronomy (the text says 'all the book')? Because we can hardly think that the men of Juda would have remained spellbound if he did. Was the people's decision put to the vote? If so, would a show of hands have sufficed? Or did the less gallant among those present demand a secret ballot? Provision is not made in the Old Testament for the plebiscite. But if we do not know the details of this curious meeting we know that it was not through sheer boredom that the most important part of it was carried through. The people *did* agree to the covenant—at the time. And the covenant was—for a while—kept. In the face of the critics it must be insisted that even if the people of Juda accepted the situation only because they were told to, expected to, appealed to, *they did accept it*. And that is why it is all the more depressing to find that they never really made the covenant their own as Josias had made it his own, that they never, so to speak, wove it into the fabric of their lives, priding themselves upon it, vying with one another in the observance of it, urging each other to be faithful to it, and regretting the years they had spent without its help. The people of Juda 'agreed' only to the covenant: God wanted them to live it.

Are we doing the people of Juda an injustice? No, because presumably they were sincerely pleased about everything when they came out of the Temple that morning into the noonday sun. The heads of families probably joined their enquiring groups with the gratifying feeling that they had been found worthy of the king's confidence. They had obeyed like lambs. For once they had risen to an occasion.

While the men of Juda were in this mood Josias pressed forward his reforms as hard as he could. This cooled the ardour of the reformed, and as they had obeyed like lambs, so were they now like lambs prepared to stray.[1]

[1] The passage quoted at the beginning of this section records the popularity and successful effects of the covenant. But apart from 4 Kings we have the testimony of Jeremias's sermons to show that the reforming scheme was forced upon a quickly cooling Juda. True,

V. G.

Reflections

iii

In our own lives are we not often guilty of the same conduct? We accept the covenant readily enough, but we do so in *our* terms, not God's. Perhaps we accept the covenant because we like the particular Josias who happens to be running it. Perhaps a certain aspect of the covenant appeals to us and, like the Jews, we are carried away by the colour and the music and the smell of incense. Perhaps we are pleased at having had the thing offered to us, flattered at being thought worthy of a trust. It is so much easier always to 'agree to the covenant'. To disagree sometimes calls for far greater virtue. The real self says one thing and the superficial self says another. And the more we are influenced by the superficial, the less easy it is for us to tell what is the real. And the less easy it is, too, for the real to find expression. Time, however, brings reality to the fore: we can bluff ourselves for a while—as we can bluff our friends for a much longer while—but we cannot bluff ourselves, our *real* selves, for ever. Our characters— what we have made of them—will eventually assert

we may justifiably assume that Jeremias, if anything, under-estimated the success with which the word of God 'was received' in Jerusalem. But even allowing for the prophet's sense of personal failure, and granting that his view of the situation was coloured by the hostility which was directed towards himself—apart from the movement with which he had identified himself—he probably *was* right in adopting a sceptical attitude towards Juda's conversion. The conclave in the Temple was not purposeless by any means: it gave Josias the impetus he needed, and it put the way of grace before those who were willing to walk by it; but, as a representative decision, the choice made on that occasion was not as significant as Josias thought it was. Thus the Book of Kings and the Prophecy of Jeremias should be read as correctives of each other. At the time of writing *Prophets and Princes* (pp. 82-88) I had not, I regret to say, studied Jeremias.

themselves. Decisions may be meritorious (or the
reverse), but it is the sustained will to abide by them
that matters. In the case of the Jews, subsequent events
showed that they had taken up the covenant as a recrea-
tion rather than as a re-creation. They showed—not
for the first time and certainly not for the last—that
they were like the younger son in the parable: 'He
answered and said I go, and he went not.' It is a sad
thing to trace the course of those who have risen in the
morning to meet the light of grace and have then gone
back to bed again. Their sleep can never be quite the
same. A good intention revoked is a lasting irritant.

The instinctive reaction of the emotions, then, are of
little importance when compared to that final click of
the will which determines the response to, or the repu-
diation of, grace. Very often our first reply to the call
of grace—as to the call of temptation—is elicited from
that part of us which is not by any means the most
characteristic. These first replies have to be reversed
later on. It means that we have been giving a *sense*
answer to a question which should properly have been
weighed in the soul. Sometimes such answers are given
deliberately—the haste being part of an absurd idea that
the real self must be prevented from committing itself—
but are subject to alteration in proportion to the
penetration of truth. Pronouncements which are flung
off while the emotions are still at play are always
liable to be recalled by the will. So a man's 'inclination' may well, when unchecked by his resolution, be
more of a hindrance to him than a help: it hinders
him from knowing his true self.

It was this, presumably, which caused the confusion
between principle and practice in the case of the two

young men in the parable: the father's request was answered before it had sunk in. 'Son, go to work in my vineyard. And he answering said, I will not. But afterwards being moved with repentance he went. And coming to the other he said in like manner. And he answering said, I go, sir. And he went not.' Each one's prompt reply meant absolutely nothing. Neither man had given his will to the business. It was not so much that they *changed* their minds, as that they did not know them.

The aphorism 'It's the intention that counts' is always being quoted to us, but if it meant that the intention alone counted, then all praise would be due to the son who said: 'I go, sir', and went not. Desires are excellent things—in fact they condition the spiritual life—but they must not be mere wishes in disguise.

The conclusion to be drawn from all this is one of encouragement. We need not, that is, assume that we are as bad as our impulses would lead us to believe. 'I am delighted with the law of God according to the inward man,' says St Paul, 'but I see another law in my members, fighting against the law in my mind.' And we must remember that the 'law of God' and the 'law of the members' are brought more nearly to the notice of the soul when God is calling it to sacrifice. Our instinctive 'No', then, can—by the grace of God—be translated into a reflective 'Yes'. (Just as the instinctive 'Yes' of the Jews was finally replaced by a decided 'No'.)

·　　　·　　　·　　　·

The sun has set behind a Jerusalem that is wearing its best robe and is eating its fatted calf: the Prodigal (to change from one parable to another) has returned.

Somewhere behind those lighted windows in the palace
Josias is dreaming and making plans; like the father in
Our Lord's story, he must wipe from the memory of
Juda those years spent 'in a far country', those years of
pleasure and of shame. Somewhere else, possibly in the
Temple or in the grotto which bears his name to this
day, Jeremias is praying for the people he loves. Like
the elder brother, he hears the music and the dancing,
but, unlike the elder brother, he is not angry in the
least; he loves the prodigal people too well for that.
Jeremias knows that men must make merry and be
glad when he that was dead is come to life again, when
that which was lost is found. The only question is *has*
Juda come to life again? *Is* Juda found?

CHAPTER VII

REMAINING YEARS OF JOSIAS'S REIGN

i

A GLANCE at the synopsis which is printed at the end of this book will show that the material for this phase of the prophet's career will exhaust itself with the nineteenth chapter of the Prophecy; from chapter twenty onwards the sermons and events belong to later reigns. The question as to where the material for this phase may be said to begin is almost as easy to determine; even without the help of a commentary most people would find, reading from chapter six (where we left off) to nineteen, that the Prophecy seems to pull up short at chapter eleven; the text shakes itself and begins again. The reason for this is surely to be found in the events described in the foregoing study of events. The finding of the Law made almost as much difference to Jeremias's work as it did to Josias's. Chapter eleven, then, can be assigned to the time immediately following the covenant episode—so at the end of 621 B.C. or the beginning of 620.

'The word that came to Jeremias from the Lord, saying: Hear ye the words of this covenant, and speak to the men of Juda and to the inhabitants of Jerusalem. And thou shalt say to them: Thus saith the Lord the God of Israel: Cursed is the man that will not hearken to the words of this covenant

which I commanded your fathers in the day that I
brought them out of the land of Egypt.'

Up till now Jeremias had confined himself to attacking such abuses as would call for correction on any showing—Deuteronomy or no Deuteronomy—here he takes
up the rôle of champion of the covenant. It is as if a
Nonconformist were to take his stand by the decrees
of the Council of Trent.

It is probably to this period that we can attribute the
earliest of those persecutions which were to make the
rest of Jeremias's life in Judea more or less of a misery.
Authorities seem to put down the hostility to a time
before the finding of Deuteronomy, but surely what the
prophet then endured was the opposition of the Anathoth
community only. Certainty cannot be reached on the
point; all that would be claimed here is that if Jeremias
was persecuted pretty generally *before* 621 B.C., then
there was far more provocation for it after. But to
resume.

Jeremias became, from 620 until the close of Josias's
reign in 609, an itinerant preacher of the Law. Judea is
not a large country, and the prophet probably found that
he could get over most of it by making his headquarters
at Jerusalem and spending no more than a night or two
away at a time. Only once do we come upon any hint
that he absented himself from the heart of Judea for
what might have been a considerable period; this is
when he seems to have travelled from Jerusalem to
Babylon and back. The account is as follows:

'Thus saith the Lord to me: Go and get thee a
linen girdle; and thou shalt put it about thy loins
and shalt not put it into water . . . and arise, go

to the Euphrates and hide it there in a hole in the rock. And I went and I hid it as the Lord commanded me. And it came to pass after many days that the Lord said to me: Arise, go to the Euphrates and take thence the girdle . . . and I went to the Euphrates and I digged and I took the girdle out of the place where I had hid it; and behold the girdle was rotten, so that it was fit for no use.'

The reason why it has been said above that Jeremias *seems* to have travelled to Babylon is because most commentators think that he almost certainly did not. The story is supposed by some modern critics to be a literary device resorted to on account of the moral which is pointed to in a later verse. Other writers prefer to think that a 'Euphrates' must have existed in the neighbourhood of Jerusalem. Each view conveniently explains away the necessity of walking the 250 miles which separated Jeremias from the Euphrates of Chaldea. On the other hand, the possibility of a visit to Babylon— and not to a local 'Babylon' in Judea on the banks of a local 'Euphrates' already referred to—is rendered all the more probable in view of the kind treatment Jeremias was later to receive when the Babylonian monarch entered Jerusalem. We shall see Jeremias and Nabuchodonosor meeting almost as old friends. But quite apart from these reasons we like to think of Jeremias telling the truth in ordinary terms, and not so veiling the facts as to provide his public with a literary fancy. We like to think of him setting out on his journey at the bidding of the Lord. He does not know how he will get there, nor does he know how—if ever—he will get back. He knows only that the Lord will manage these things. We like to think of Jeremias, after enduring every conceivable hardship on the road and enjoying every conceivable adventure, *actually* digging in the bank of Chaldea's river and hiding his belt in a hole. There is something highly unsatisfying about the suggestion that the whole thing is to be taken figuratively and that the prophet was digging with the inspired word for the hidden heart of Juda. We far prefer to think of him digging with a spade. 'Behold the girdle was rotten, so that it was fit for no use.' We see the prophet pulling up a sodden, muddy, worm-eaten waste-band, and listening to the Lord's explanation of the symbolism: 'After this manner will I make the pride of Juda to rot . . . for as a girdle sticketh close to the loins of a man, so have I also brought close to Me all the house of Israel . . . that they might be My people, but they would not.'

Whether or not Jeremias undertook the journey he mentions, it is clear that the lesser journeys—in and about Judea—which he took at about this time were attended by hardship and adventure. The lot of itinerant preacher is an unenviable one in any case, but it must be especially so when the public addressed has begun to feel the sting of a guilty conscience. In Judea the first flicker of enthusiasm had died away by this time, and the 'covenant' was already more of a reproach than an inspiration. Jeremias, when not being hounded from village to village, would have had to nurse the dull ache of disappointment. It is awful to think of the sensitive Jeremias as the object of cheap ridicule and bitter comment. Crowds that have hardened their hearts are very much the same whether they happen to come from Benjamin or Bermondsey: Jeremias, like many a prophet since, was made miserable by the thanklessness of his task. 'And they obeyed not, nor inclined their ear, but walked every one in the perverseness of his own wicked heart. And I brought upon them all the words of this covenant which I commanded them to do, but they did them not.'

This statement seems prompted by a scene—perhaps quite a few scenes. Behind the words we seem to hear hoots and hissings and the cry (hurled after the prophet as he is chased along the dusty road) that he can preach his precious covenant elsewhere.

For ten years he was to endure this sort of thing, and possibly for longer.[1] The time would come later on when Jeremias would gradually, and under the guidance of God, begin to shed what might be called the textbook side of Deuteronomy and supply a more directly spiritual doctrine of his own. God teaches His children first to fear the Law and then to love it. Jeremias had to begin his instructions rod in hand; it was time enough in after years to substitute the crutch. 'Perfect love casteth out fear', but 'the beginning of wisdom'—and therefore of Love—'is fear'. Later, when Josias his friend is dead, the prophet will still wander abroad in his devoted advocacy of the word, but it will be in an advocacy of the word made flesh and not of the word made stern.

[1] Particularly objectionable to him would have been the intensified hostility of the Anathoth priests. These, trained in the Abiathar tradition, would have resented the monopoly of worship which Deuteronomy gave to the Zadokite clergy in Jerusalem; that Jeremias was pressing for this would have added to their grievances against him.

ii

Having gone rather fully into the repercussions of the discovery of Deuteronomy, it would be as well to say something about the work itself. A mere paragraph will suffice to show the divisions into which it naturally falls (and by glancing at the chapter headings the matter can be further subdivided), whereas the question of its origins can be treated somewhat more carefully; problems of authorship are always less dull than the arrangement of material. In what follows no original conclusions will be found as to either division, date or authorship; we hold simply to the Catholic tradition—namely, that the Book is what it claims to be: the testimony of Moses.

As regards the splitting up of the text, then, we can note the four main ideas running through the whole:

First, the insistence on the Godhead's Unity and supremacy (as compared with the multitude of 'other gods' worshipped by the peoples of contemporary civilisations; see vii, 21; x, 12; vi, 15; vii, 12, 13).

Second, the corporate character of Israel's worship (vii, 6-8; ix, 29; xxvi, 18, 19).

Third, the necessity of a single centre of worship, the Temple. (This was to insure against local cults which had a tendency to deteriorate into superstition, and then finally into idolatry.)

Lastly, the need to supply subjects for the priesthood from a single tribe only. It was these last two points which so infuriated the Anathoth community; they were no longer able, under the covenant, to maintain their individuality as an exempt and rather rare body.

For further analysis Fr Hugh Pope's frequently cited

'*Aids*' (Vol. 2, pp. 69-79) should be consulted. The writer brings out the fact that Deuteronomy—in contrast to Exodus and Leviticus—was a book for the layman rather than the priest; 'It shows the people,' says Fr Pope, 'the responsibility incumbent upon them of keeping the covenant established between God and themselves . . . the legislation is set out with greater clearness and precision than in the earlier books.' Thus the layman was taught to contribute individually (by his own personal sanctification) towards the sanctity of the race.

From what has been said it can be seen at once how appropriate was Deuteronomy to the present need. *So* appropriate, in fact, that certain critics claim that it was conveniently 'discovered' to meet that need. This brings us to our second point, the question of Deuteronomy's authorship. Here we have the higher critics at their best—they give us an evening paper headline, WHO FORGED THE BOOK OF THE LAW?

Professor Lods discusses the matter in his capital book *The Prophets and The Rise of Judaism* (pp. 144ff.), and much interesting speculation is put forward in Dr Cheyne's *Jeremiah: His Life and Times* (pp. 66-81). The case as made out by those who do not follow the Catholic tradition on the point is roughly this: Since the only people who stood to gain by the discovery were Josias, Helcias, Saphan and Jeremias, *and* since the same people were by virtue of their position easily able to cover up their tracks, *they* and not the scribes of Moses—as has been believed for upwards of four and twenty centuries—were the joint authors of the Book of Deuteronomy.

Josias is suspect because from the moment of his

accession he had been looking out for a good excuse to reform Juda. He was not a strong enough character to pull up the nation on his own account, and the Law was just the thing he needed. The 'testimony of Moses' would carry a conviction in the statutes which 'the will of Josias' would not. Let Moses, then, be caused to leave a testimony. A case of Mahomet and the mountain—only now it was the mountain and Moses.

Helcias is suspect because it was he who 'found' the document in question. The critics, be it noted, assume that the account in 4 Kings is a true record of events as far as the writer was granted to see their outward course. On the theory that the high priest was the forger, the Book of the Law is not to be attributed to the other characters as well, but simply to the one man; the rest are exonerated as having lent their weight in good faith to the movement which resulted.

Saphan is next suspect because he, as a scribe, would have known how to fake a text. In his dealings with manuscripts and on account of his unquestioned access to the libraries, Saphan would have had ample opportunity of working upon the spurious document without fear of interruption or supervision.

Jeremias, lastly, is suspect because, of the many sacred writers who appear to have drawn inspiration from Deuteronomy, he, the rigid reformer, is the most conspicuous. Jeremias, it is argued, wrote both books: the Law and the Prophecy. He used the Law to gain the Prophecy a hearing and he used the Prophecy to expound the Law. Though not strictly taking away the character of the Inspired Word, this theory takes pretty well everything away from the character of the inspired writer.

All that can be said is that if Jeremias (or any of the other fellow suspects) forged Deuteronomy, he certainly did it very well indeed. *So* well as to deceive all save the rationalist critics of a few years ago. He managed to get himself back into the legislative, social, and ecclesiastical atmosphere of seven hundred years before his own time, and to do it in such a way that no contemporary was able to detect anachronism or deceit. Let a present-day writer attempt the same experiment. Let one of our textual critics make a study of Elizabethan literature, let him steep himself in Elizabethan politics, let him familiarise himself with the moves of Elizabethan churchmen, let him penetrate that strange thing the Elizabethan conscience, let him do all this and then let him pass off a forgery with success. The years, moreover, which separated Moses from Jeremias are more than double the years which lie between Elizabeth's time and ours.

It is true that the arguments against Deuteronomy being contemporaneous with Leviticus are somewhat compelling,[1] but the arguments against it being a work of the seventh century B.C. are (to my mind) stronger still. The fact that Divine Providence brought Deuteronomy to light at the moment when it was most wanted is exactly what we would expect of Divine Providence. And yet it is this fact which sends off the critic, magnifying-glass in hand, to look for other explanations, however unworthy. The critic—especially if he calls himself a higher critic—should instead be on his knees giving thanks to God for having stepped in precisely when He did. If we try to detect a criminal beneath the hairshirt of the prophet we are not likely to benefit

[1] See Cheyne, op. cit. pp. 70-75.

in soul from our searching of the Scriptures. The excuse
that an 'innocent deception only' is laid upon the
consciences of the reformers is no excuse at all. It is
positively asserted by one of these kindly excusing
commentators that Helcias's object was to terminate
the painful hesitancy of those who believed in a spiritual
religion by producing a law-book which should represent
the divinely appointed ordering of church and state;
Helcias thus 'interpreted' the mind of Moses. But surely
this was very wrong of him? Oh, no, says the kindly
critic; he had the highest motives, and besides, people
judged things differently in those days. I submit that in
'interpreting the mind of Moses', Helcias was presumably interpreting the mind of Jehovah as well.
'Harmless error'—is all that I can find in justification—
'is to be tolerated in the interests of purer truth.' The
term 'pur*er* truth' is puzzling. But in any case for a
man to sit down and write a book which is to be pub-
lished under someone else's name and which sets out
to rank as revealed Scripture is not to 'tolerate a
harmless error', it is to do something highly immoral
and sacrilegious.[1]

[1] It should be said here that there is yet one more theory as to
who was responsible for the forging of the Law: the Temple priests
are charged with practising the innocent little deception. The reason
given is the desire for gain. They thought (it is alleged) that if
worship were confined to the one spot, Jerusalem, and that if the
priesthood were recruited from the single tribe (their own—that of
Zadok), then the community which served the Temple would be in
a very strong position indeed. This is all quite true, but it leaves out
of account the fact that the Book of Deuteronomy could be used—
and *was* used with great effect by Jeremias—against the Temple
clergy as well as against the priests of Juda's outlying districts.
We have seen as much on an earlier page, and shall return to the
same theme when dealing with the effect of Jeremias's preaching
in a later reign. 'The prophets prophesied falsehood,' says Jeremias,
'and the priests clapped ther hands.' This was said before the
finding of the Law; Jeremias had declared himself, then, an anti-

iii *On legislation*

It might reasonably be asked by anyone studying this section of the Prophecy why Jeremias, already a deeply spiritual person and obviously on the way to heroic sanctity, laid such stress upon keeping to the letter of the law. Surely he must have known that the essence of true religion lay more in the inward than in the outward ordering of man's life? And since Deuteronomy never pretended to be anything else but a code or legislative system, could not Jeremias have taken liberties with its decrees in order to enclose a wider harvest of souls? Had not his message from the Lord been delivered in broader terms—'if you oppress not the stranger and the widow, and shed not innocent blood I will dwell with you in this place'?[1] The answer to this difficulty might be found in the purpose of law

clerical. But what about after the finding of the Law? We examine his sermons and find that his attitude is strengthened; he is in a better position than ever for attacking the priests. He puts the covenant before the Temple clergy, before the Anathoth community and before the faithful at large. He is told that his mission-field is to be the 'cities of Juda' and the 'streets of Jerusalem': the Lord wants all to hear His words. And they are strong words indeed: 'Woe to the pastors that destroy and tear the sheep of my pasture. . . . I did not send prophets, and yet they ran; I have not spoken to them, and yet they prophesied . . . they prophesy falsely in My name; and I have not sent them, saith the Lord.' Thus the priests had nothing to gain by the promulgation of Deuteronomy as commentated upon by its chief propounder. Nor, of course, had the chief propounder anything to gain—humanly speaking—by propounding it.

[1] vii, 6, 7. See also ix, 24; v, 28; vi, 20. Each of these citations comes from Jeremias's pre-Deuteronomy period. It is worth noting that a change of tone is discernible by the time Josias comes to die: in the prophet's panegyric (xxii) Josias's highest virtue is his readiness 'to judge the cause of the poor and the needy.' We might have expected that the sovereign's chief claim to immortality lay in his observance of the Law. Perhaps Josias's love for God's word is taken for granted; at any rate, it is for his charity that Josias is praised by the prophet.

in general—as distinct from this particular code of laws which we have been considering.

With the discovery of Deuteronomy Jeremias was granted to see, in a way he had never yet seen, what rules were really *for*. In enforcing the covenant he was not so much pressing a yoke upon Juda's neck as providing the easiest way of getting Juda's feet out of the mire. The Book of the Law was *liberative*. Jeremias was not trying to wrench a headstrong race to an older and stricter observance, he was trying to train up a very silly race in a clear-cut service of its Lord. Jeremias knew well enough that rules were the framework only and not the work itself, but he knew also that where there was no frame there was likely to be—in the case of the Jews particularly—no work.

That is why the saints have made so much of religious observance. St Teresa had no need to stop talking at the sound of the bell in order to keep herself recollected; she knew very well, however, that if bells were not taken seriously in the Carmel a whole train of consequences would follow: conversations would be prolonged, duties would be neglected, silence would be undervalued, and the grace of contemplation would be less freely granted to the Order. We need a frame. We can sometimes step out of it for a little while, but it is not safe to remain outside it for long—particularly if the frame is quite clearly ours by God's appointment.

Thus laws are worthy of their name only when they free the subject from a tyranny more cramping than the yoke of legislation. A religious takes his vows knowing that he will find a greater liberty in his cloister than he could possibly find in the world: he will—if he is faithful to his vocation—no longer be a slave to any earthly thing. So the religious who jumps over his convent wall in order to be free is no more achieving his object than a fish which jumps out of its tank in the Brighton Aquarium: each is making the mistake of wanting an element which is foreign to its nature. Legislation which is *purely* prohibitive is meaningless: legislation *must* develop *some* things—or at least keep the subject away from others. We do not restrain ourselves for the sake of restraining ourselves; we restrain what is evil in order to train what is good. An educational system which would rule out certain studies, certain games, certain books, without either showing why they were to be avoided or providing others in their place, would be a very bad one indeed. This is why laws, when once they fail in their main purpose, are found to do more harm than the evil itself would have done which they were intended to correct. Before promulgating a law a legislator should make quite certain that it will work. Nor is it only when the legislation is rejected and disobeyed that the consequences are liable to be disastrous; law which is misunderstood is also capable of developing the very qualities which are most at variance with it. Thus you get misinterpreted Deuteronomy producing, in the time before the coming of Christ for instance, a blind pharisaism: the letter killing instead of quickening. Thus you get misinterpreted charity producing lust instead of love; misinterpreted hope producing presumption instead of trust; misinterpreted faith producing fatalism instead of effort. It is awful to think that the means chosen by God to free a man from his selfishness can be twisted by man to be the means of his deeper self-entrenchment.

The Jews, then, had to be told by Jeremias that they must revise their ideas about the worship of God. It was required of them that they worship Him in a particular way. It was the way best suited to them, besides being the way most worthy of Him. But they needed to be told also—in case they should place their trust in the way instead of in the worship—that the Law must be *lived* and not merely subscribed to as a system.

Did Jeremias succeed in bringing all this home to the Jews? We dare not pronounce. All that can be said for certain is that Jeremias was thoroughly disappointed with the results. It is curious to note that in proportion as he felt himself becoming more and more of a failure he became more and more Messianic in the hope which he held out. Roughly from chapter seventeen onwards the prophet seems to be aware of the dawn which is to follow Juda's night, until he can say with confidence in chapter twenty-three, 'Behold the days shall come, saith the Lord, and I will raise up to David a just branch, and a king shall reign, and shall be wise, and shall execute justice and judgement in the earth. In those days shall Juda be saved and Israel shall dwell securely; and this is the name that they shall call Him: THE LORD, OUR JUST ONE.'[1]

So we see how Jeremias is setting about his work: he teaches the Law by revealing the Lawgiver. He is telling the Jews that He who has breathed life into the Law will come in Person to fulfil it. If there are souls in Israel to whom the iron-bound Book of Deute-

[1] These two verses are taken for the 'little chapter' of Terce and Sext during the Advent season. Isaias is the prophet most represented at this time.

ronomy is either a pain on the one hand or a hobby on the other, then the Messias alone—the Word Itself—can bring to those souls the just balance of love. 'For the law was given by Moses, grace and truth came by Jesus Christ.'[1]

[1] John i, 17.

CHAPTER VIII

THE DEATH OF JOSIAS

i

THOUGH Jeremias was, as we have seen, much objected to in Juda we must remember that he still had his supporters. His father, Helcias, believed in him, and his sovereign, Josias, was directed by him. So the prophet was probably not lonely, even if he was very much alone.[1] But Helcias was not going to live for ever, and Josias was soon to be killed in war. It is this latter event which is to occupy us in the present chapter.

The last twelve years or so of Josias's reign were tranquil years for Juda; they were to end with what, to us at this distance, looks like one of the most useless battles ever fought. To account for the calamity we must watch the movements of nations outside our immediate field since the time when the Scythian disturbances were providentially disposed of.

We have seen how, already during Josias's minority, Assyria had been forced to loosen its hold on the peoples paying tribute to Niniveh. Assurbanipal, Esarhaddon's successor, was the last of Assyria's

---

[1] May we number Baruch among Jeremias's friends at this time? Or does the faithful secretary come into the prophet's life only when Josias has gone out of it? We do not know. Nor do we know if, as has been suggested, the nameless author of the first nine chapters of the Book of Proverbs was one of Jeremias's supporters and fellow workers.

effective rulers; he reigned from 668-626 B.C., dying a
year before Nabopolassar's assumption of power in
Babylon had marked the birth of the Neo-Chaldean
Empire. With the death of Assurbanipal there followed
revolt after revolt in Assyria, with the result that foreign
vassals everywhere pressed for returns of territory.
Josias seems to have been one such vassal; but though
he tried all he could to secure Juda's independence he
felt himself bound to support Assyria in the event of
third-party aggression. By the year 612 Nabopolassar
had, with the Medes to help him, begun his campaign
against Niniveh. But this was not strictly Juda's
affair, since the theatre of war was quite obviously
out of Juda's reach. Josias therefore maintained his
neutrality. It was only when, a few months later,
Egypt showed signs of coming up towards Assyria
from the south that Josias decided to defend the
crumbling empire. In 611 B.C., then, you had Pharaoh
Necho about to attack Assyria and trying to march
through Palestine to do so. Necho had no quarrel with
Juda whatever. In fact, it was in his interests to keep
up friendly relations as far as possible, knowing as he
did that the feeling in Jerusalem for the past fifteen
years had been markedly pro-Egyptian. This point
should be borne in mind, because Cheyne and others
would seem to have it that Josias lost his life in an
attempt to save his country from the ravages of an
Egyptian invasion. He did nothing of the kind; he
died in a chivalrous attempt to save the country to
which he owed fealty from being plundered by a
country with which most of Juda would have been
pleased to make an alliance. It is much to the credit
of the men of Juda that they rallied to so unpopular a

cause; Josias's idealism must have been infectious indeed.

What has been said is borne out by the accounts in 4 Kings and 2 Paralipomenon. Quoting from the last named:

> 'He [Necho] sent messengers to him [Josias] saying: what have I to do with thee, O king of Juda? I come not against thee this day, but I fight against another house, to which God hath commanded me to go in haste. Forbear to do against God, who is with me, lest He kill thee.' (And the text goes on) 'Josias would not return, but prepared to fight against him.'

This is an illuminating passage; between the lines of it we can see a great deal. We can see the young Egyptian patriot (Necho was not much older than Josias) in council with his ministers. The news has just reached him that Josias seems inclined to stand in the way of Egypt's northward march. Necho sends an appeal for Juda's neutrality. 'We don't want to alienate the sympathies of these Israelites,' Necho is telling his cabinet as the brown dust of Palestine blows in through the flap of the royal tent, 'they can be useful to us for provisions and whatnot; also we can hardly afford to lose men in an Israelite engagement before meeting the Assyrian. It will indeed be a pity if Josias clings to his fetish about fidelity to his suzerain, . . . but then he has the reputation of being a high-souled idealist. How would it be if we put the thing on a supernatural basis? take down this message and send it off at once . . . "Forbear to do against God, Who is with me . . . " '

Or are we doing Necho an injustice, and *had* God in some way communicated to him that Egypt was to march against Assyria? This is not impossible when we consider that Assyria's overthrow had been foretold and was even now due. Someone had to put the finishing touches to Niniveh's shame, and there were only Egypt and Babylon to choose from; Juda could not have managed it on her own, and the Medes were not yet in the field except as co-operators with the Persians in Nabopolassar's armies. One would have thought that of the two nations, Egypt and Babylon, the Lord would have chosen Babylon to do His work, but it may be that He was reserving this for a later date, when, under Nabuchodonosor, who succeeded Nabopolassar in 605, Babylon was to be raised to a power unequalled either in Egypt's or Assyria's previous history. However, even allowing that it *was* in the Divine plan to select Egypt for the further humiliation of Assyria ('further' humiliation, because in the event it was Babylon and not Egypt which finally reduced Assyria's capital, Niniveh, to ashes), it is unlikely that the Lord would have signified as much in so many words to Necho—unless of course Necho was at heart a believer in the God of Israel. So it looks as if we are driven to take the less charitable view with which we started, and to say that all this talk about 'God's command' was sheer hypocrisy on Necho's part. He wanted to touch Josias on what he knew was Josias's tenderest spot. 'If we cannot frighten him or bribe him,' Necho can be heard to say as the messenger leaves the assembly, 'there is one thing that we can do, and that is to talk to him about the will of God.' The ministers concur and the emperor sits down.

A few miles away Josias is making heroic and terribly sincere speeches up and down the lines of his fighting men. His audience is not enthusiastic about the proposed resistance to Egypt, but the king is so obviously keen on it that the troops would not dream of going against him. Then comes the Egyptian runner with the Necho dispatch. Josias reads the document. . . . 'Forbear to do against God,' ran the message, penned in Hebrew characters by an Egyptian hand, and 'lest He kill thee' was the reason given. Josias decided to fight. That he should 'do against God' was the last thing which he would want, that he should be killed by God's hand caused him no tremor at all.

The next thing we hear is that Josias *was* killed. Can it be that Necho knew what he was talking about after all? Whatever else is doubtful, one thing is abundantly clear: if Josias mistook God's will he mistook it in perfectly good faith. So it looks in the last analysis as if there is room in the story for sympathy with both men, Josias and Necho. Josias too eager to fight the battles of his suzerain, Necho reluctant to trample on the prince who bars his way. One would have wished that an angel of peace had swept down on to the battle ground five minutes before the clash of swords, or that a prophet (Jeremias for example—except that he was perhaps too anti-Egyptian in feeling to do it readily) had somehow prevented the encounter. The whole thing seems to have been one of history's Big Mistakes.

'But he went to fight in the field of Mageddo,'[1] (concludes the account in Paralipomenon, the writer of which was clearly one of Josias's most

[1] Mageddo is a flat piece of land about twelve miles north of Nazareth, at the foot of the Samaritan hills.

ardent admirers), 'and he hearkened not to the words of Necho . . . and there he was wounded by the archers, and he said to his servants: Carry me out of the battle, for I am grievously wounded. And they removed him from the chariot into one that followed after him, after the manner of kings, and they carried him away to Jerusalem, and he died and was buried in the monument of his fathers. And all Juda and Jerusalem mourned for him; particularly Jeremias, whose lamentations for Josias all the singing men and singing women repeat unto this day.'

It is at least gratifying to know that Juda mourned generously. Once he was no longer at their doors, urging them to keep promises which they had done their best to forget, Josias became a sort of holy legend. Juda woke up to the fact that it had been governed for the last thirty years by a saint. But taken all in all, they were not for going back upon the past; the 'covenant' was a mistake—however worthy the man who made them take it up. Only fitting to shed tears in honour of Josias's shade, but it would be most uncomfortable to have him back again.

'Particularly Jeremias' mourned for the dead king. We are not surprised. For one thing Josias had given his life in a vindication of the prophet's anti-Egyptian policy, and for another he happened to have been Jeremias's friend. The prophet, walking beside the bier of the king as the procession made its way to the monument of Juda's royal dead, would have had much to occupy his thoughts. He remembers what Josias looked like as a boy, when he, Jeremias, used to come up for

the day from Anathoth to witness a pageant or a
military review. He remembers Josias as the young
reformer, as the devout worshipper, as the faithful
husband and father, and as the lifelong student of the
Law which it has been his mission to enforce. And
then there are the clear-cut memories of these last
few days, memories which will be with the prophet
until he dies. He sees again the litter as it is borne
through the southern gate of Jerusalem; he hears the
hoarse voice of his friend urging Juda to a greater
act of faith; he mingles with the group of courtiers
and physicians who stand, helpless and silent, beside
the bed of the dying king. (Who, we wonder, were
present for this? Helcias the priest—very old by now—
was he there? Saphan the scribe? Some of Josias's
worthless sons?) Jeremias remembers how clipped
and jerky were Josias's final utternaces, and how
inconsequent they were in the heat of fever; he watches,
over and over again, the sick man's heaving effort
to breathe . . . until, the intervals lengthening between
the gasps, there is the silence of—literally—the dead.
The twitching fingers have relaxed, the roving, un-
seeing eyes have found a new focus, the beads of
sweat have dried upon the body that can no longer
bear the flame of life. Jeremias goes out on to the
terrace and hears from there the news proclaimed that
one king is dead and that another has taken his place.
Yes, he recalled it all, all the details of these recent
happenings, none of it—from the murmur of dismay
that had gone up from Jerusalem when the first runner
had come from Mageddo's field down to the clean
crisp notes of the silver trumpets which only this
morning had summoned all Juda to the burial—would

be forgotten by the man who claimed to be the dead
man's friend.

ii

Alongside these personal considerations Jeremias
would have mourned the loss as affecting the fate of
Juda. He saw, as no one else in Jerusalem saw, that
now would come the final test of Juda's character.
Would the nation rise above the disaster, acknowledg-
ing the present calamity to be a just punishment for
its sins? Or would Juda sink further into the mire of
idolatry, judging that the God of Israel had played
His people false? On the answer depended, incidentally,
the prophet's future. But his prospects under suc-
ceeding kings would have given Jeremias little cause
for either speculation or anxiety: with him it was the
fate of Juda that mattered, not the fate of Jeremias.
The Holy City, the Chosen Race, the Temple of
Jehovah, the Book of God's Law . . . what would
become of them all in the next few years?

CHAPTER IX

THE REIGNS OF JOACHAZ AND JOACHIM

i

FROM the foregoing chapter we see that the warnings of Jeremias were amply justified: Egypt had again proved a disastrous element in Juda's history. But just as Assyria—in accordance with the prediction of Isaias—had been overthrown, so now Egypt would in its turn be brought to destruction—in vindication of Ezechiel's and Jeremias's words—by the power of Babylon. Nabuchodonosor undertook to drive the southerners out of Palestine and was entirely successful. But this was not until the battle of Carchemesh, in 605 B.C., when Necho's dream of spreading Egypt's influence over what is now known as Asia Minor was finally shattered. So with Syria, Assyria and Philistia (all the then-known Eastern world, in effect, with the exception of Juda), under Chaldean dominion it was only to be expected that Babylon should cast envious eyes on Jerusalem. Babylon did; and it was Jerusalem's rejection of Babylon's overtures which caused her to lose, in the next twelve years, most of her wealth, most of her nobility, most of her prestige and no less than three kings.

Following the death of Josias:

'Joachaz was three and twenty years old when he began to reign and he reigned three months

in Jerusalem . . . he did evil before the Lord
according to all that his fathers had done. And
Pharaoh Necho bound him at Rebla, which is in
the land of Emath, that he should not reign in
Jerusalem. And he set a fine upon the land of a
hundred talents of silver and a talent of gold.'

So for three months Joachaz had the time of his life.
This was in 609 B.C. He was not Josias's eldest son,
and consequently had no right to the throne; he seems
to have been put on because he was popular with the
masses.[1] It is curious to note that Necho allowed
Juda to elect its own sovereign; at all events he soon
regretted his generosity, because he got rid of him
almost at once and appointed his own nominee, the
rightful heir, Eliacim. Joachaz was 'bound at Rebla'
and sent off to Egypt, where he would be out of the
way. (One suspects that Joachaz had been discovered
in some sort of secret negotiations with Babylon.)
Rebla (not mentioned in Paralipomenon) was evidently
the city at which Necho's armies were quartered during
the campaign. Joachaz was accompanied into exile
by his mother; he died a few years later and does not
come into the story again. He is referred to by Ezechiel
(who does not, however, mention his name) in terms
which bear out what Jeremias had to say about him.
Joachaz need concern us no more.

[1] It is to the chronicler of Paralipomenon that we owe this piece
of information (2 Par. xxxvi, 1). The new king's name was Sellum
as well as Joachaz; Jeremias addresses him as Sellum when prophesying evil to his house (xxii). This seems to have been the only
occasion when the prophet had any dealings with the king. The
chapter is in the wrong place, coming as it does after a passage
treating of Sellum's next successor but one. Since there is no action
in the chapter, and since it adds little to the prophecies discussed
elsewhere in this book, I am presuming to leave it out altogether.

So we see that Jeremias's worst forebodings were speedily realised: Juda, following the lead of its king, sank back again into sin. The chapters in the Prophecy which are assigned to this period are full of dooms and woes. As had been feared, the Jew argued along lines which were as entirely false as they were entirely unanswerable. Prosperity in Josias's day, they reasoned, had been due to the secret cults of gods whose patronage had never wholly been cast off; Josias (himself good, zealous, public-spirited and patriotic, but utterly misguided in his religious outlook) had been struck down by the jealous deities to whom his monotheism had been obnoxious; if the gods were now suitably appeased there was every hope that Juda would eventually enjoy immunity from Egypt, Assyria and Chaldea. But this would take time; the immediate need was to pay off Necho. Let the Pharaoh have his Joachaz, and let him take his tax of the Temple treasury . . . and as for the policy of the future, let there be no more talk of the 'covenant of the Lord'.

Equally unproven, of course, would be the opposite reasoning—the reasoning which was to be heard night and day from the lips of Jeremias: Juda had lost her battle and her king because of the secret idolatries which had still endured, and the peace which Juda had enjoyed for the past thirty years had been a sign of God's favour—the reward for what little obedience had been rendered to His commands; the present duty therefore was clear—obey the commands more fully and keep the covenant. But this line of argument did not appeal: the conscience of Juda was asleep.

ii

With the deposition of Joachaz we make the acquaintance of Josias's eldest son, Eliacim. The accounts of this man's reign are almost identical in both authorities, Paralipomenon and Kings; we quote from Paralipomenon because it is shorter.[1]

> 'And he [Necho] made him [Eliacim] king in his stead over Juda and Jerusalem, and he turned his name to Joachim; Joachim was five and twenty years old when he began to reign and he reigned eleven years in Jerusalem. And he did evil before the Lord his God.'

Necho's high-handed treatment of Eliacim is evidence of the confidence he had in his position: for one monarch to change another's name shows power, particularly if the new name signifies a new relationship. 'Joachim' means 'servant of Pharaoh'—a post which was lived up to with some fidelity. 'And Joachim gave the silver and gold to Pharaoh'—this is from the other source, the Book of Kings—'after he had taxed the land for every man to contribute according to the commandment of Pharaoh.'

Not chosen by 'the people of the land,' as his brother had been, Joachim (to call him, as we shall do from now onwards, by his imposed name) treated 'the people of the land' outrageously. Not merely on the word of Paralipomenon and Kings do we know this; Jeremias and Ezechiel say the same. Jeremias's

---

[1] The parallel passages are: 4 Kings xxiii, 34—xxiv, 5; and 2 Par. xxxvi, 4-8.

F—j

twenty-second chapter is mostly about the enormities which were practised in this king's reign.

Shortly after his accession Joachim seems to have rebelled against 'Nabuchodonosor, king of Babylon, and became his servant three years'. This must mean that the fealty which he owed to Necho was shortlived and that Nabuchodonosor took over the peoples which had been paying their dominion dues to Egypt. This rebellion, which ended in Joachim's service to Babylon's king, should not be mistaken with the second rebellion, which ended in Joachim's exile. The second was a far more important occasion, because it spelled at the same time the complete overthrow of Egypt, with which Juda was at that time allied. Having fought against Egypt in 609 Jerusalem was sending out men by the hundred in 605 to support the armies of Pharaoh. But the combined effort which was to force Chaldea back to the Euphrates came to nothing; Necho and Joachim were up against Nabuchodonosor. Carchemesh (605 B.C.) virtually settled Egypt's and Juda's destinies for the next fifty years. Joachim's fate was much the same as his younger brother's had been: he was bound and led in chains to the country of his captors—in this case to Babylon. We are told in the account of Joachim's deportation that Nabuchodonosor carried away also 'the vessels of the Lord and put them in his temple'; he took at the same time a number of Juda's nobles and a certain proportion of the state treasury. This was the thin edge of the captivity wedge—a wedge which was to separate two of Juda's major prophets from their native land. Daniel and, some years later, Ezechiel were victims of Nabuchodonosor's justifiable anger against Jerusalem's royal and unreliable house.

In justice to Joachim it must be said that he had no easy task when he came to the throne: his brother had been worse than useless, and coming as he did with a bare three months separating him from his father's godly rule, it was in the full flood of a reactionary backwash that he took over the helm. The reign opened with confusion in Juda. The twenty-fourth chapter of Kings gives a brief account of the harryings which Jerusalem endured from her neighbours at this time, and concludes with the words: 'This came by the word of the Lord against Juda to remove them from before the face of the Lord for all the sins of Manasses which he did.' But in spite of the evils which handicapped Joachim's assumption of power all would have been well had Jeremias's advice been acted upon. The prophet told Joachim to yield to Babylon. Joachim would not listen. Jeremias then appealed to both Joachim's ministers and Joachim's subjects, in the hope that the king would be forced to take his advice. The result was, as we shall see, that instead of having only the king against him he had also the ministers and the people against him; he was nearly killed for his pains. Joachim threw in his lot with the man whose servant (as his name testified) he was, and so backed, with the erring judgement of the amateur gambler, the wrong horse. It had been the favourite horse for a long time past, but, as Jeremias was never tired of pointing out, its racing days were over. Joachim lost all that was left to him of kingship and died in misery and exile, unmourned by his people and without hope from his allies. The sons of Josias are hardly showing themselves equal to their father's lead.

Having gone some way ahead of the story, we can

now examine what Jeremias was saying and doing in the years following Josias's death. The interlude of Joachaz's rule was of such short duration that it can be linked to the rule of Joachim.

iii

If Jeremias lacked public confidence before Juda's defeat at Mageddo he certainly lacked it after. No longer enjoying the patronage of the ruling sovereign, his position in Jerusalem was hardly safe. As seen through the eyes of the nationalist, Jeremias appeared to be not only a very bad prophet, but a very bad patriot. Had he not warned Juda that Scythia would overrun the land? Had he not said that all would be well if the Jews observed the Law? And what was the result? The Scythians had been turned back and the observance of the Law had been rewarded with the death of Josias. And here he was now—urging submission to Babylon! What would the diehard Isaias have said to such a policy? Better the easy yoke of Egypt than extermination at the hand of Nabuchodonosor.

With the nearer approach of Nabuchodonosor would come the need for the 'traitor's' suppression: his propaganda value was high enough to make him a dangerous man in Jerusalem. The cry 'Away with him' was raised—as it was raised against another and an even greater Prophet—and Jeremias walked in danger of his life.

It is impossible, in the absence of direct allusions to contemporary events, to assign for certain any of the prophet's sermons to the time we are considering. We are probably safe, however, in saying that chapters sixteen, seventeen and eighteen belong here. There is a certain unity about them which inclines to the idea that they were composed under the influence of a single mood—a chastened mood at that. Fortunately the man is not dominated by the mood. The hopelessness which the prophet seems to have felt is countered by the naked faith which he had learned from God in prayer. He already knew at this time that the whole of his vocation rested on what he was not able to feel, but what he was able—just—to believe. Such were roughly the terms of the original engagement: 'They shall fight against thee and shall not prevail, for I am with thee, saith the Lord, to deliver thee.' To 'deliver thee', the Lord had said, not to 'appear to thee'.

The prophet was first of all told that he must never marry. The Lord seems to have wanted rather to save Jeremias trouble than to mortify him.

> 'Thou shalt not take thee a wife, neither shalt shalt thou have sons and daughters in this place. For thus saith the Lord concerning the sons and daughters that are born in this place, and concerning their mothers that bore them, and concerning their fathers of whom they were born in this place: They shall die by the death of grievous illnesses; they shall not be lamented and they shall not be buried; they shall be as dung on the face of the earth.'

The implication seems to be that the young women of Jerusalem were such a bad lot that a marriage from among their number would not only hamper Jeremias in his prophetical ministry—as in the case of Osee the minor prophet—but would, on the purely human plane, prove more of a burden than a blessing.

Is the wistful note which is discernible throughout these three chapters due, one wonders, to the prophet's compulsory bachelorhood? Surely not. It is hard in any case to imagine Jeremias as a family man. The depression is due much more to the swinging back of the religious pendulum—to chaos and to the sudden rush after strange and lying gods.

Not only was Jeremias forbidden to marry, but he was also told to go no more 'into the house of feasting, to sit with them that eat and drink'. The prohibition sounds severe. 'Behold I will take away out of this place,' the Lord went on to say, 'the voice of mirth and the voice of gladness, the voice of the bridegroom and the voice of the bride.' Whatever else this passage tells us, it certainly shows that all these joyful things have been enjoyed by Jeremias at one time. Time was —and, but for the Lord's veto, would be—when invitations to weddings were readily accepted. Hard as his lot had been from the moment of his call, there had remained to Jeremias the power to be glad. Otherwise the power would not now be mortified by a direct injunction from the Lord. Notice that the word 'mirth' is used, suggesting downright gaiety. Now that you are entering (says the Lord) upon a new and somewhat grimmer phase of your career, these social consolations had better cease; from this time onwards you will be able to say: 'Thy word alone will be to me a joy, O Lord, and gladness to my heart.'[1]

Thus there does seem to be evidence in support of

[1] xv, 16.

the thesis outlined above, namely that Jeremias was
no misanthrope. The fact that people can cry is
reason to believe that they can laugh. Jeremias himself understood this. He told the people[1]—speaking
this time in the person of the Lord—that the 'virgin
of Israel' would come into her own once more: 'Thou
shalt again be adorned with timbrels, and shalt go
forth in the dance of them that make merry.' Tears
are for a time only. 'Rejoice ye in the joy of Jacob,
and neigh before the head of the Gentiles. Shout ye
and sing . . . ' The idea of *neighing* is a curious one;
perhaps it has something to do wlth laughing at the
enemy's cavalry attacks; at any rate, it suggests a
certain hilarity. The timbrels, again, are unquestion-
ably instruments of joy. It is a pity they are no longer
used: a timbrel is a far more cheerful instrument than
a saxophone. 'They shall flow together,' prophesies
Jeremias of the built up race, 'to the good things of
the Lord, for the corn and wine and oil . . . and their
soul shall be as the watered garden, and they shall be
hungry no more.' But the best is yet to come, for
'Then shall the virgin rejoice in the dance, and the
young men and old together; and I will turn their
mourning into joy and will comfort them and make
them joyful after their sorrow.' It is a happy Jeremias
who is speaking, a Jeremias who can look beyond the
tragedy of Josias's death and out into a country full
of sunshine, where there is no idolatry and no persecution of prophets. The conclusion of the passage is
quite as gay: 'Let thy voice cease from weeping and
thy eyes from tears, for there is reward for thy work,
saith the Lord, and there is hope for thy last end.'

[1] xxxi, 4, 10, 13 ff.

More restrained, but not less jubilant, is the heralding, three chapters later, of the Messias. 'I will make
the bud of justice to spring forth unto David'—Jeremias is speaking again, of course, in the person of the
Lord—'and He shall do justice and judgement in the
earth. In those days shall Juda be saved and Jerusalem
shall dwell securely. And this is the name that they
shall call Him, THE LORD OUR JUST ONE.'

There is no mistaking this. The Rising Sun of
Justice has, in anticipation, brought the glow of early
morning to the leathery cheeks of the man of tears.
'I will bring back their captivity,' is the Lord's last
word, 'and I will have mercy on them.' As the prophet
lays down his pen he finds that his whole being is
flooded with the warmest pleasure . . . he will not mind
the loss of married life, of feasting and of song; he has
found—in its beginnings, at any rate—what his soul
has been looking for.

To return to the three chapters which we set out to
examine, 'The sin of Juda,' says Jeremias when he has
told of the Lord's commands as regards himself, 'is
written with a pen of iron, with the point of a diamond,
it is graven upon the table of their heart, upon the
horns of their altars'; and there follows a colourful
picture of the self-sufficient materialist, 'the man that
trusteth in man and maketh flesh his arm, and whose
heart departeth from the Lord'. The punishment
reserved for such is 'to dwell in dryness and in a salt
land'. The picture is complete: you have the epicure
being made to rough it. Thirsty and uncomfortable,
the *bon viveurs* and the dilettantes are left with a salty
taste in their mouths and nothing to look at but a
desert waste. Far different is the lot of 'those who

trust in the Lord', of whom the prophet is able to say: 'he shall be as the tree that is planted by the waters. . . it shall not fear when the heat cometh . . . as the partridge hath hatched eggs which she did not lay: so is he that hath gathered riches, and not by right. In the midst of his days he shall leave them . . .'

Commentators would have it that Jeremias borrowed all this from other writers. What if he did? It shows, at any rate, that he had an ear for the music of words. With the fourteenth verse of this chapter (the seventeenth) the tempo suddenly changes, and you have the old, somewhat querulous, Jeremias back again: the prophet is seen to be shrinking, in the lower part of his soul but not in the higher, from his task. 'I have not, Thou knowest,' he cries out in his prayer to the Lord, 'desired the day of man . . . be not Thou a terror unto me . . . let them be confounded that persecute me . . . let them be afraid and let not me be afraid.' This is the Jeremias of twenty-five years ago. And how frank of him to admit it! The man who has served the Lord for a quarter of a century is trying to back out before he is let in for another quarter of a century's service. Rather, he is *wishing he could* back out: he must know that his real self has chosen for good—literally for 'good'. He is merely allowing his natural self to have its say. 'Let this chalice pass from Me' is echoed in the agonies of the saints who have come after Christ and anticipated in the agonies of those that have gone before. And always the clause following is added, speaking of the soul's surrender to the Father's will: 'yet not as I will, but as Thou wilt.' 'I have not desired the day of man,' says Jeremias in his Gethsemane, and then in the verse following, 'Thou art my hope in the day of affliction.'

iv

In the last of these three chapters, which I have
ventured to attribute to the year 608 or thereabouts,
we get the account of Jeremias's visit to the potter's
shed.

> 'The word that came to Jeremias from the
> Lord, saying: Arise and go down into the potter's
> house, and there thou shalt hear My words. And
> I went down to the potter's house, and behold he
> was making a work on a wheel. And the vessel
> was broken which he was making with clay with
> his hands, and turning he made another vessel
> as it seemed good in his eyes to make it. Then the
> word of the Lord came to me saying: Cannot I
> do with you as this potter, O house of Israel?
> Behold as clay is in the hand of the potter, so
> are you in My hand, O house of Israel.'

The whole thing in six verses—a bare two inches of
print!

We can see the prophet setting out at the bidding
of the Lord. He wonders what will be told him when
he gets to the potter's house. Will he be required to
apprentice himself to a trade? Is the potter himself a
prophet? Will he find in the potter's shed a band of
souls who will form the nucleus of a 'remnant people'?
Jeremias arrives, and stands at the open door of the
potter's house. He watches the age-old industry. He
studies the craftsman as he builds up a shapeless clay
mound on the smaller of two wheels, he sees him work
the lower and heavier wheel with his feet, he stands
fascinated by the sight of the potter's hands as they

shape the clay . . . and still he wonders why the Lord
has sent him here. The potter detects a flaw in the
surface of the vessel he is moulding. The wheels are
brought to a halt. The work is scrutinised. Over
goes the faulty vessel on to the heap of shards! Another
vessel is begun . . . another flaw . . . again the pile of
broken bits is added to. This goes on for perhaps half
an hour. At last comes the reward in the shape of some
really sound material. Ah, that's better . . . just the
right consistency . . . what shape would the man of
God like it to be? *Any* shape did he say? How about
this? Just *one* moment . . . great care must be taken
over the finishing touches. There! *Flick*, and the
pitcher is whisked off the wheel to be exhibited to the
prospective purchaser, who has been leaning all this
time against the uprights of the potter's doorway.
But the prospective purchaser is looking strangely
absent-minded. 'Cannot I do with you, O house of
Israel? . . . ' The word has come to the prophet Jeremias.

.　　.　　.　　.　　.

The wheels are still spinning, the flies are still wrig-
gling in the wet clay on the potter's bench, the potter
is still wondering what to make of his preoccupied
visitor. . . .
Turning from the shade of the potter's house,
Jeremias strides out into the fierce glare of the sun
outside. And as he walks home to his rather cheerless
abode he wonders within himself how best he can
deliver himself of the message of the Lord.

.　　.　　.　　.　　.

As things turned out, the prophet must have delivered himself of the Lord's message with some heat,

because his hearers seem to have been cut to the quick. But instead of deciding to do better, the house of Israel decided to despair. 'And they said: We have no hopes, and we will do everyone according to the perverseness of his evil heart.' This, of course, made Jeremias miserable and very angry. Justifiably so. It was, however, the less attractive side of Jeremias which cried out to the Lord (in the concluding verse of the chapter we have been considering), asking that 'their sin be not blotted out from Thy sight; let them be overthrown before Thy eyes; in the time of Thy wrath do Thou destroy them.'

CHAPTER X

THE TOPHETH AFFAIR

THE prophet's nineteenth chapter is the practical working out of the lesson which he was granted to learn in the potter's shed. It tells of another object-lesson, but this time it is Jeremias who does the teaching. The same moral and the same material as in the previous chapter are repeated here, and so we are probably correct when we claim that this section of the Prophecy follows closely upon the heels of what we have just been dealing with. It is as if Jeremias, having delivered his message according to instructions and having met with nothing but disappointment, was urged to take up the potter-and-clay story and to go on with it where it had been left off.

> 'Thus saith the Lord: Go and take a potter's earthen vessel, and take of the ancients of the people and of the ancients of the priests, and go forth into the valley of the son of Ennom which is by the entry of the earthen gate, and there thou shalt proclaim the words that I shall tell thee.'

Carrying his earthenware pitcher, Jeremias would have made his way straight to the Temple, where, having assured himself that the 'ancients of the people and the ancients of the priests' were well represented, he would have placed himself in a conspicuous position. He was fairly certain of a hearing. The rather bored

Temple-goers were always willing to listen to one whose violence complemented their own lassitude. This morning there was the usual crowd; some hurrying in and out of the Temple, others content to lean or squat against the Temple wall. In addition to the worshippers there would have been the pedlars, the sellers of cooling drinks, the money-changers, the pigeon-vendors, the basket-makers, the carpet-menders, the seedy little groups of brokendown scribes and itinerant schoolmasters . . . all getting what shade they could as they either sat or shuffled about in the great open arch of the Temple gate. Into this throng came Jeremias with his earthenware jug. Heads turned to look at him. The spitting and joking and nudging and gesticulating ceased as the prophet took stock of the material at hand . . . would he ever be able to fashion a vessel from such clay?

The prophet at this time was in his late forties, but we imagine him looking older. We think of him as having skin like dried tobacco-leaf and eyes that take fire at the slightest provocation. His figure is so spare that one expects to hear his bones rattle when he walks. His head and feet are uncovered; he wears the camel-hair dress of the more 'advanced' prophet. He has a voice like the copper gong of the Temple; and his beard has long been innocent of the comb.

'Come forth into the valley of the son of Ennom,' is the prophet's invitation. They come forth. Heading the procession Jeremias strides out of the city in silence by way of the 'earthen gate'.[1] The people are

[1] This was also called the 'sherd gate' by reason of the broken pottery which was thrown there as rubbish. Was the route so chosen by the Lord with the intention of still further stressing the significance of broken vessels?

a little self-conscious as they thread their way, to the huge enjoyment of the onlookers, through the narrow, crowded, noisy streets . . . there is giggling and horse-play on the part of the light-minded, and dark looks and scowls from the 'ancients'. Heads are mopped, eyes are shaded, garments are gathered up from the ankle, and the expectant congregation pushes on. Fortunately the valley of the son of Ennom is no distance from the city walls; they reach the place in a matter of minutes.[1] Once arrived and settled into some sort of order, the people prepare themselves to listen. They are slightly uneasy—not so much on account of what Jeremias might have to say as on account of what the Jewish civil authorities might have to say. The site of this strange assembly is a sinister one, and has unpleasant associations: it has been used for false worship and for unlawful gatherings of every kind. However, now that Jeremias has brought his congregation here, the best thing is to stay and see the thing through. The people look at the prophet and wait. Then it comes—torrents of it!

'Thus saith the Lord of hosts, the God of Israel: Behold I will bring an affliction upon this place that whosoever shall hear it both his ears shall tingle . . . the days will come when this place shall no more be called Topheth nor the valley of the son of Ennom, but the valley of slaughter.

[1] 'Narrow, with steep and rugged rocks on either hand, the valley formed a natural defence of the city on the western and southern sides, joining the eastern valley of the Kedron.' (Streane, *Jeremiah and Lamentations*, p. 69.) It is believed that children were sacrificed in this locality; the name 'Topeth' or 'Topheth,' which comes in the next citation, is supposed to be the Aramaic word for 'fire-place'; the word can also mean 'place of shame'. (See Peake, *Commentary on The Bible*, p. 480.)

I will defeat the counsel of Juda and Jerusalem
in this place, and I will make this city an astonishment and a hissing.'

But this is only the beginning of what Jeremias has
to tell the people. He is merely pausing for breath
when he says that the Lord will make His Holy City
an astonishment and a hissing. The place Topheth,
within hailing distance of Jerusalem's walls, must be
washed clean of its sin in the blood of Sion's citizens.
Jeremias is pointing over the heads of his audience to
the capital which must expiate its crimes. He takes
a step forward on his rocky platform. His right arm is
jerked to shoulder height . . . and then high up over
the broken horizon an earthen bottle is seen spinning
against the blue of a cloudless sky. *Crack*, and it
smashes to a thousand pieces on the boulders of
Ennom's amphitheatre. And before the men and
women have turned their eyes again to the preacher—
'*So* will I break this people and this city, saith the
Lord . . . ' The prophet's voice is caught by the surrounding rocks and hurled, echoing, strident, compelling, into the midst of Juda's priests and people.

I have quoted only a verse here and there, but the
whole passage is deserving of study. Especially interesting is the fact that the sermon did not end where it
began—Jeremias went on with it when the crowd got
back again to the city.

'Jeremias came from Topheth, whither the Lord
had sent him to prophesy, and he stood in the
court of the house of the Lord and said to all the
people: Behold I will bring upon this city all the
evils that I have spoken against it because they

have hardened their necks that they might not hear My words.'

We wonder what was in men's minds as the procession made its return journey through the 'earthen gate'. Had souls been stirred at all? Or had they been moved only to anger? At any rate, we can be fairly sure that there was no giggling or horse-play in the narrow and dirty streets of the capital. There may possibly have been—on the part of some—the hush of respectful awe, and there almost certainly were bitter resentment and threatening looks, but, whatever else, the burning words of Jehovah's messenger were this time taken seriously.

CHAPTER XI

THE SEQUEL TO THE TOPHETH SERMON

'Now Phassur the son of Emmer, the priest, who was appointed chief in the house of the Lord, heard Jeremias prophesying these words. And Phassur struck Jeremias the prophet and put him in the stocks that were in the upper gate of Benjamin, in the house of the Lord.[1] And when it was light the next day, Phassur brought Jeremias out of the stocks.'

THIS is a quotation from the prophet's twentieth chapter; we must continue with the text in a moment.

It seems then that the act of finishing his discourse in the Temple precincts so infuriated the authorities that Jeremias was arrested. He had preached in the Temple before, but never had he gone so far as to pronounce a curse upon the Holy City. The night spent in the stocks had, as we shall see, a curious effect upon Jeremias. The place was a more or less public one, and the presence of aggressive guards, deeply wounded priests, indignant citizens and mocking casual loungers, was enough to discourage the bravest of confessors of the faith. The faces of his tormentors, seen in the fitful light of guttering torches, would have suggested to Jeremias that not for much longer would he rank among

[1] This is not one of the gates of Jerusalem; it is the northern entrance to the inner court of the Temple. See 4 Kings xv, 35, where it is mentioned as having been built in the reign of Joatham.

God's confessors—the title 'martyr' appeared to be drawing near.

In the early morning Phassur came in person to release the prisoner. Perhaps he had acted in passion the night before and had left out some of the formalities. Another interpretation of Phassur's action, however, will be suggested below. Certainly the proceeding has the appearance of being somewhat irregular, and the last thing the church wanted was to fall foul of the law. In the grey half light of dawn Phassur approaches Jeremias with keys in his hand and a look of uncertainty in his eyes. Jeremias has spent the best part of a sleepless night in framing what he will say to Phassur when next the two men meet. He says it.

> 'And Jeremias said to him: The Lord hath not called thy name Phassur, but Fear on Every Side. For thus saith the Lord: Behold I will deliver thee up to fear, thee and all thy friends; they shall fall by the sword of their enemies, and thy eyes shall see it. And I will give all Juda into the hand of the king of Babylon, and he shall carry them away to Babylon and shall strike them with the sword . . . thou, Phassur, and all that dwell in thy house shall go into captivity and there thou shalt be buried.'

Did this grim and personal forecasting of doom come true? One somehow hopes not, but there is no reason to expect that Phassur escaped the fate which was certainly in store for many of his fellow priests. At all events, the rest of this prophecy, the part about 'all Juda', was strictly fulfilled. The speech to Phassur over, Jeremias's words undergo a sudden change.

Addressing himself to the Lord, he is found to have
lost all that confidence and sureness with which we
have just heard him speak. The text goes on:

> 'Thou hast deceived me, O Lord, and I am
> deceived. Thou hast been stronger than I, and
> Thou hast prevailed. I am become a laughing-
> stock all the day. All men laugh at me. For
> I am speaking now this long time, crying out
> against iniquity and often proclaiming devasta-
> tion, and the word of the Lord is made a reproach
> to me and a derision all the day.'

Another fit, we say, of the prophet's despairing
gloom. Here I must interrupt the story to make a
personal observation. When I came to this part of
the text I was so puzzled by the abrupt change over
from one emotion to another that I decided to say
nothing about it. It was only when I read on and
found exactly the same sort of thing in chapter twenty-
six that I decided to investigate further. I discovered,
to my great satisfaction, that the two chapters described the same event. The joy of making this discovery was equalled only by the joy of discovering how
the two accounts dovetailed into each other. The fact,
which was subsequently revealed, that others had made
the first discovery before me in no way lessened the
pleasure of having found out how the two chapters could
be re-written as one. The result of this splicing process
may be found at the end of this book in an Appendix.

If we return to the text which we have interrupted
we find that the prophet, having told the Lord how
miserable he was, changed back again to his mood of
joy; verse thirteen reads as follows:

'Sing ye to the Lord, praise the Lord because he hath delivered the soul of the poor out of the hand of the wicked.'

Then the rebound once more:

'Cursed be the day wherein I was born; let not the day in which my mother bore me be blessed . . . why came I out of the womb to see labour and sorrow, and that my days should be spent in confusion?'

This is obviously something different from a mere wave of general despondency which is followed by another mere wave of shallow trust. There must be some explanation of these fluctuating sentiments. The explanation which I venture to submit does not so much account for the play of Jeremias's temperament as fill in the gaps of Jeremias's account. The sudden contrasts are better understood when we have formed a more complete picture of that night in the stocks. And for this we shall need the text of chapter twenty-six:

'The priests and the prophets and the people heard Jeremias speaking these words in the house of the Lord. And when he had made an end of speaking all that the Lord had commanded him to speak, the priests and the prophets and the people laid hold on him, saying: Let him be put to death. Why hath he prophesied in the name of the Lord, saying: This house shall be like Silo and this city shall be made desolate without an inhabitant? And all the people were gathered together against Jeremias in the house of the Lord. And the princes of Juda heard these words, and they went up from the king's house into the

house of the Lord and sat in the entry of the new
gate of the house of the Lord.[1]   And the priests
and prophets spoke to the princes and to all the
people, saying: The judgement of death is for
this man, because he has prophesied against this
city, as you have heard with your ears.   Then
Jeremias spoke to all the princes and to all the
people, saying: The Lord hath sent me to prophesy
concerning this house and concerning this city
all the words that you have heard.   Now, therefore, amend your ways and your doings, and
hearken to the words of the Lord your God; and
the Lord will repent Him of the evil that He hath
spoken against you.   But as for me, behold I am
in your hands, do with me what is good and right
in your eyes.'

As this is a stopping place in the prophet's speech it
may also serve as a place where we can pause to make
our reconstruction of the night's happenings.

Jeremias had just come back, we remember, from
the Topheth sermon. He had repeated parts of it in
the presence of the high priest himself.[2]   Whereupon,
as we have seen, Phassur struck him in the mouth and
had him put in the stocks.   In all this (here we turn
to the second account) Phassur had the clergy and the
people on his side; 'let him be put to death' was as
popular a cry in reference to Jeremias as was 'crucify
Him, crucify Him' in reference to Our Lord.   During

---

[1] The secular authorities went *up* because the Temple was on a
higher level than the palace buildings. They sat in the Temple's
gateway because 'such a place as this was the ordinary one for
trials'. (*Streane*, op. cit. p. 182.)

[2] There appears to be some doubt as to Phassur's office (see
Binns, p. 106). If he *was* the high priest at this time then it means
that Helcias was dead; this may account for the lack of support
to Jeremias's cause.

the night (again from the later chapter) a number of
things took place: the secular authorities got to hear
about the matter; a meeting was convened within the
Temple enclosure, during which the 'princes' listened
to the accusations brought by the clerical body. On
the charge of having blasphemed against the Holy
City Jeremias was found guilty and sentenced to death.
As soon as it was morning Phassur (we are back again
now at the first quotation) arrived at the stocks and
prepared to release the prisoner. Phassur's part in the
business was over; he came now to hand over his man
to the secular arm. It is here that the solemn cursing
of Phassur and his house took place. Now, then, with
the night of physical and mental strain at the back of
him, with the effort of having cursed a high priest,
with the thought that he was now being led out to die,
the prophet's energy was spent. He collapsed. He
reproached God in his prayer. Notice that there was
no *outward* sign of weakening—he was to take up his
stand again in a few minutes without an atom of dis-
composure—it was *within* that Jeremias allowed his
doubts to manifest themselves. 'Thou hast deceived
me, O Lord, and I am deceived. I am become a laughing stock . . . ' and now I am going to die without ever
having realised the vocation which You guaranteed for
me. (We can now leave the first account until almost
the close of the incident.)

Either at the actual place of execution or still within
the walls of the Temple precincts Jeremias made his
declaration before the princes and the people of Jerusalem. He fully believed that it was going to be the
last time he would address his fellow Jews. He was
determined to make the most of the occasion. He
gave the reason for his having prophesied in the first

place.   He then appealed to Juda to amend.   And
lastly he left himself in the hands of his judges.   'Do
with me what is right in your eyes'—whatever happened, it would be according to God's will.   The 'princes'
were impressed.   The 'prophets' were impressed.
The 'priests' were impressed.   The 'people' also were
profoundly moved.   Jeremias saw this and decided to
go on with his address.

> '*But*,' (he said) 'know ye and understand that
> if you put me to death you will shed innocent
> blood against your own selves . . . for in truth the
> Lord sent me to you to speak all these words in
> your hearing.   Then the princes and all the people
> said to the priests and to the prophets: There is no
> judgement of death in this man, for he has spoken
> to us in the name of the Lord.'

By this time the issue of the thing was almost assured.
Notice that it was the prophets and the priests who had
to be persuaded of Jeremias's innocence; it was they
and not the princes or the people who had been responsible for the indictments.   Notice also, of course—
though one can hardly help noticing—how closely the
whole account resembles the account of another trial,
a trial which was as unjustified as Jeremias's, but
which had different results . . . results which amounted
to deicide.

There is a wealth of interest in the last phase of the
incident:

> 'And some of the ancients of the land rose up,
> and they spoke to all the assembly of the people,
> saying: Micheas of Morasthi was a prophet in the
> days of Ezechias king of Juda, and he spoke to
> all the people of Juda, saying: Thus saith the

Lord of hosts: Sion shall be ploughed like a field and Jerusalem shall be a heap of stones, and the mountain of the house [i.e. the Temple] shall be the place of woods. Did Ezechias king of Juda, and all Juda, condemn him to death? Did they not fear the Lord and beseech the face of the Lord, and the Lord repented the evil that He had spoken against them? Therefore we are doing a great evil against our own souls.'

And so it was that Jeremias was acquitted. Phassur and his crowd of jealous priests must have looked distinctly at a disadvantage, but apart from them the incident is much to the credit of the men of Juda. Particularly is it to the credit of the 'princes', who were able to quote their case-law with effect. Micheas had certainly provided precedent, but one would hardly have expected the ill-instructed aristocracy of Joachim's court to have known enough of church history to cite it.

We can easily reconstruct the finish of the episode. As far as Jeremias goes we have his own words to help us to do this. 'Then Jeremias said: Sing ye to the Lord; praise the Lord because He hath delivered the soul of the poor out of the hand of the wicked.' (This, it will be remembered, is taken from the earlier chapter —the passage which seemed, on account of the sudden contrasts, so unsatisfactory as a full record of events.) The prophet, then, was happy in his release. We picture him returning to his modest apartment in the town surrounded by a little group of men and women who have hitherto feared to be associated with his work. For a while, at all events, Jeremias will be free to preach God's message . . . and the happenings of last night have taught him that his preaching was not in vain. The princes, who had shown such admirable discretion over the whole affair—summoned though they had been from their very beds to judge the case—in all probability went off together to celebrate their one and only forensic triumph with a meal. And what of the people of Juda? Wayward, sensation-loving, fair-weather-friendly, the Jews probably went home wondering if this had not perhaps been a sign that they must amend their lives after all.

That night, under cover of darkness, any preparations that had been made earlier on in the day for a public execution were discreetly covered up. Among the servants of the Crown there were doubtless some slightly treasonable jokes as well as some bitter reflexions about the high priest Phassur and his friends. There was probably speculation, too, as to how long Jeremias would remain immune from further attack. A sound man (Jeremias would have been voted) thus to have scored off the least loved body in the realm.

'Struggle, man against man, defiance: a splendid rebel . . . ' we are back again at the type provided for us by Mr Morton. Jeremias has shown us that, whatever was going on within his own soul in the way of natural shrinking and fear, he was unwavering in the direction of his conduct . . . 'away from compromise, away from surrender', into a land where he could take pain and pleasure equally at the hand of God.[1]

[1] I should perhaps add, before closing this section for good, that not all commentators would agree to the linking up of Jeremias's twenty-first chapter with his twenty-sixth. A number of authorities refer the second account to a quite different sermon. Thus the arrangement of texts which will be found in the Appendix is conjectural only.

CHAPTER XII

FURTHER INCIDENTS IN JOACHIM'S REIGN

i

A S MAY be gathered from the foregoing, Jeremias was not, except at rare intervals and with the very few, popular in Jerusalem during the miserable reign of Joachim king of Juda. Hitherto we have considered the prophet's dealings with Joachim's subjects, here we can consider the prophet's dealings with the king.

> 'Thus saith the Lord: Go down to the house of the king of Juda, and there thou shalt speak this word.'

This is a verse from the prophet's twenty-second chapter. The passage represents a collection of prophecies subsequently edited and put into the text without particular connexion with what has gone before or with what comes after. The chapter and the three chapters following are not remarkable, so we need delay only so long as they afford us a glimpse of the line which Jeremias saw fit to take at this time with his sovereign. In most outspoken terms Jeremias reproached the king to his face for neglecting the necessities of his people while adding to the luxuries of his palace. Jeremias further pointed out the difference between existing conditions in Juda and the happy state of affairs which had prevailed during Josias's

term of rule. As a punishment for his mismanagement
and rapacity Joachim would, Jeremias told him, die
unmourned by relatives and subjects alike, and would
be denied even the honour of being buried. We are
not told how Joachim received all this, but we are told
(on other pages of Scripture[1]) that these predictions
were exactly verified.

Whether at the same interview or at another,
whether in a private audience or in a public place,
Jeremias expanded his attack into a denunciation of
unworthy rulers in general. This is his twenty-third
chapter. 'You have scattered My flock,' was Jeremias's
message from the Lord, 'you have driven them away
and have not visited them; behold I will visit upon
you the evil of your doings.' But there would dawn a
day of universal remedy: the Just Judge would rule
where the unjust had usurped their power.

With Jeremias's twenty-fourth chapter we have the
welcome introduction of a vision. 'The Lord showed
me, and behold two baskets of figs set before the
Temple of the Lord . . . one basket had very good figs,
like the figs of the first season, and the other basket
had very bad figs, which could not be eaten.' The
account is deliciously naïve. It goes on: 'And the Lord
said to me: What seest thou, Jeremias? And I said:
Figs; the good figs very good, and the bad figs very
bad.' The explanation, granted then and there to the
prophet, was simple enough. The first lot of figs
represented the exiles of the captivity, the second
represented the Jews who would remain. Thus again
we find the prophet's anti-Egyptian attitude reinforced
by the Lord: of those that remained under Sedecias in

[1] Jeremias xxxvi, 30; 4 Kings xxiv, 6.

Jerusalem a great number were to find their way to
Egypt never to return. Those, on the other hand, who
went into exile with Joachin and Daniel and Ezechiel
were able to maintain some sort of unity as Hebrews
and finally to return again from Babylon to their native
land.[1] And in point of fact the whole future of Judaism
was committed to the basket of good figs, while the figs
in the other basket went from bad to worse. This
mention of the Babylonian captivity provides Jeremias
with the opportunity of proclaiming the future supremacy of Babylon; his twenty-fifth chapter is about the
power which Nabuchodonosor will wield over the then
known world, and the decline of this power under subsequent Chaldean rulers. This brings us to the twenty-
sixth chapter, which, it will be remembered, we anticipated in order to supplement the night-in-the-stocks
chapter (the twentieth).

ii

Though having no direct bearing upon the life of
Jeremias, there is an incident recorded in this section
of his Prophecy which it would be a pity to leave out.
Incidentally it brings Joachim into the picture, and so
is not out of place in a chapter which intends to treat
of the king as well as the prophet.

'There was also a man that prophesied in the
name of the Lord, Urias the son of Semei of Cariathiarim. He prophesied against this city and
against this land according to all the words of
Jeremias. And Joachim and all his men and all

[1] Ezechiel endorsed Jeremias's view of the contrast; see xi, xvii.

his princes heard these words, and the king
sought to put him to death. And Urias heard it
and was afraid, and fled and went to Egypt.'

Urias is believed to have been a follower of Jeremias.
Nothing is known of his father, Semei. Cariathiarim,
the spot where the Ark of God had rested for twenty
years,[1] is a city on the borders of Juda and Benjamin,
about ten miles north-west of Jerusalem. The man
seems to have been perfectly genuine, but timorous.
When he heard that an order was out for his arrest
he decided, with Jeremias's narrow escape from an
exactly similar circumstance in mind, to move south.
As it happened, Urias could hardly have chosen a
worse country in which to take refuge: Egypt and Juda
were at this time still united in the bonds of closest
friendship. Necho would have been only too pleased to
effect the return of a fugitive; had Urias fled to Egypt
two or three years later, he would have been kept
there as a prisoner. But as it was:

'Joachim sent men into Egypt, Elnathan the
son of Achobor and men with him. And they
brought Urias out of Egypt and brought him to
king Joachim. And he slew him with the sword
and cast his dead body into the graves of the
common people.'

It is a grim little interlude in the story, and one
wonders at first why it was put in at all. The verse
which follows provides the clue. 'So the hand of
Ahicam the son of Saphan the scribe was with Jeremias
that he should not be delivered into the hands of the
people.' Surely the 'so the hand of Ahicam,' etc.

[1] I Kings vi and vii.

indicates that poor Urias's fate was the warning which sent Jeremias into temporary retirement. A 'splendid rebel' Jeremias still was, but in the interests of his fellow rebels he had to be kept in hiding for the time being. Ahicam the son of Saphan saw to that. Saphan was probably dead by this time or he would have sheltered Jeremias himself. There is something particularly pleasing in the thought that Saphan, the friend of Helcias, should have left behind him sons who were not afraid to look after Helcias's son. This Ahicam, whose guest Jeremias was during the months following Urias's death, had been a member of the deputation which was sent by Josias to the prophetess Holda fifteen years previously. He must have been a very young man then. We shall see later on in the story that Ahicam's sons, Godolias and Gamarias, showed in their turn the same hospitality to their father's and their grandfather's friend. Jeremias owed much to Saphan's family.

The other name mentioned in the above extract, Elnathan the son of Achobor, also appears later on as being one of the king's advisers. On the next occasion he will figure as a man of moderate views.[1] Over the Urias affair he had probably no chance of making suggestions. His father, Achobor, had been another of those who had consulted Holda, so it looks as if Joachim had taken over his father's cabinet as it had come to him in 608 B.C. The incident of Urias further shows that whatever the king thought of Jeremias there were certain among the 'princes' who valued him in the kingdom. It was the princes, we must remember, and not the king, who had judged in the prophet's

[1] xxxvi, 25.

favour against Phassur. It was only a pity that the same men were not able in the case of Urias to quote the same precedent. Joachim was taking no risks this time: he would conduct the whole matter himself, and there would be no talk at all about his ancestor Ezechias and the Micheas reprieve. 'He slew him with the sword,' is the obituary notice of the timorous but genuine Urias, 'and cast his dead body into the graves of the common people.' One's heart bleeds for the timorous but genuine Urias; he would have been so much happier if he had followed Jeremias's example. If a man must be a rebel, the only kind to be is a splendid one.

iii

The next event which comes up for consideration is taken from the Prophecy's thirty-sixth chapter. The chapters in between this and those which we have just been examining belong to later dates, and so need not be dealt with yet. At present we are concerned with an episode which took place after Carchemesh and before Joachim's ill-starred rebellion against Nabuchodonosor. It is an episode which introduces, at long last, the secretary and chronicler Baruch.

'The word of the Lord came to Jeremias, saying: Take thee a roll of a book and write in it all the words that I have spoken to thee against Israel and Juda and against all the nations from the days that I spoke to thee, from the days of Josias even to this day. If so be that when the house of Juda shall hear all the evils that I purpose to do unto them they may return every man from his wicked way, and I will forgive them their iniquity and their sin. So Jeremias called Baruch the son of Nerias, and Baruch wrote from the mouth of Jeremias all the words of the Lord which he spoke to him on the roll of a book.'

Professor Wheeler Robinson, writing for Peake's *Commentary*, says of this passage: 'The failure of the oral testimony led to its preservation through writing. The pioneers amongst the so-called "literary" are not primarily writers at all; the written records of their work are largely incidental, a fact which helps to explain the fragmentary and complex character of much of the prophetic "literature", due, as it largely is, to the work of disciples.' So it looks as if this is the first attempt on Jeremias's part to publish the word of God apart from the pulpit and platform. Nor was it only that he wanted his sermons preserved to posterity—he probably left that part of his mission to the designs of Providence—he wanted to see to it that the present generation should have no excuse for evading revelation:

'And Jeremias commanded Baruch, saying: I am shut up and cannot go into the house of the Lord; go thou therefore and read out of the volume which thou hast written from my mouth the words of the Lord in the hearing of all the people in the house of the Lord on the fasting day.'

Let us get quite clear the setting of this event. Jeremias had been preaching submission to Babylon. The armies of Babylon were at no great distance from the walls of Jerusalem, and Nabuchodonosor had already begun to suspect that Joachim was not as

loyal as he might be. Jerusalem was becoming alarmed.
A fast had been proclaimed throughout Judea, possibly
to meet the present danger and possibly (if Streane's
conjecture is correct) to mourn the anniversary of
Carchemesh. Frightened evacuees were hurrying into
the capital from the outlying cities and villages in
Judea in order to shelter behind the walls of the Holy
City. The opportunity, therefore, of addressing an
unusually large assembly in the Temple was a unique
one: the people were receptive and possibly even
conscience-stricken. But Jeremias was 'shut up' and
could not preach. What does this 'shut up' mean?
Some commentators say that Jeremias was in prison,
others that he was merely suspended from preaching.
In view of the effect of Urias's execution it seems more
likely that Jeremias was still enjoying the hospitality
of Ahicam and was persuaded by his host not to show
himself in public until the Babylonian issue had settled
itself one way or the other. Unable to attend in person
Jeremias sent his deputy. A word on the prophet Baruch.

Baruch was a scribe who seems to have had some
sort of standing at court before throwing in his lot
with Jeremias. He was the grandson of Maasias the
'governor of the city', who is mentioned in 2 Paralipomenon as having been sent, together with Helcias
and Saphan, to see to the repairs of the Temple in
Josias's reign.[1] Baruch's brother was Saraias, whose
office was to be 'chief over the prophecy'—whatever
that meant—and who was companion to Sedecias on
the occasion of the latter's journey to Babylon.[2]

[1] 2 Paralipomenon xxxiv, 8.
[2] Jeremias li, 59. Other texts have for 'chief over the prophecy'
the equally enigmatic phrase 'prince of the camping place'. Whatever
the duties, the title was evidently one which commanded respect.

The world of Juda's nobility must have been a very small one, everybody seems to have been related to everybody else. Thus Baruch was a man who could take his place with the princes who had shown favour to Jeremias in the past. That the favour was extended to the secretary as well as to the prophet will be shown in the episode which we are about to consider. It would appear from a later chapter in the Prophecy (the forty-fifth chapter to be precise) that Jeremias found Baruch to be a little too forthcoming: the prophet had occasion to reprove his secretary for a want of humility. But whatever else, Baruch was loyalty itself as regards Jeremias, and the work of acting as scribe to a voluminous prophet for upwards of twenty years can have been no sinecure. The late Dr Cheyne is right when he refers to the 'brave and faithful Baruch'.

> 'And Baruch the son of Nerias did according to all that Jeremias had commanded him, reading out of the volume the words of the Lord in the house of the Lord.'

And nothing happened! It is odd, but there is no mention whatever of the effect which this first reading had upon the people of Juda. Were the fasting multitude apathetic? Had they heard this sort of thing so often that they could no longer bring themselves to listen with unhardened hearts? Did some of their number—not enough to make it worth the prophet's while to record the fact—repent? There is no means of knowing; the text reads straight on:

> 'And it came to pass in the fifth year of Joachim son of Josias king of Juda, in the ninth month, that they proclaimed a fast before the Lord to all

> the people in Jerusalem and to all the people
> that were come together out of the cities of Juda
> to Jerusalem.'

This is so like the account of the previous occasion
that one might almost think that the repetition was
due to a printer's error. Baruch was told to do exactly
the same thing again. He must have shrunk from the
commission if the first rehearsal had been a failure.
But perhaps that is why the first rehearsal *was* a
failure—to show to forthcoming prophets what prophets must expect. Anyway, there is one detail which
characterises the second reading: the detail as to where
the meeting exactly took place.

> 'And Baruch read out of the volume the words
> of Jeremias, in the house of the Lord, in the
> treasury of Gamarias the son of Saphan the scribe,
> in the upper court, in the entry of the new gate
> of the house of the Lord, in the hearing of all the
> people.'

One or two minor difficulties are presented by this
extract; commentators have not so much as mentioned
them. First, how did 'all the people' fit into the
treasury which was presumably an ante-chamber or
hall leading off one of the Temple courts? Again, if
'all the people' were there, why was not Gamarias there
himself? It was *his* treasury. As a matter of fact he was
attending a council-meeting at the palace while Baruch
was speaking. And if there was a council-meeting
going on at the palace it means that the important
people of Juda were all of them absent from the reading
of the roll. I would suggest as a tentative solution that
Gamarias (who, it must be remembered, was the

son of Ahicam, the protector of Jeremias) *chose* the time of the council-meeting to lend his hall for the furtherance of the prophet's plans.   There was no reason why he himself should be there, since he probably knew all that was contained in the roll already, and there was every reason why his fellow-councillors should be kept away.   The princes had shown themselves sympathetic once before, but there was no reason to believe that they would take such a reasonable view of the present scheme.   With regard to the other difficulty—how to put all the people into the treasury—I submit the suggestion that Baruch spoke from the balcony of Gamarias's apartment to the people, who were assembled in one of the Temple's courtyards below; the text distinctly says that the treasury was in the 'upper' part of the gate, and if the people were massed in the space about the gate itself there would have been room for a considerable crowd.[1]

'And when Micheas the son of Gamarias the son of Saphan had heard out of the book all the words of the Lord, he went down into the king's house to the secretary's chamber.   And behold all the princes sat there: Elisma the scribe, Dalaias the son of Semeias, and Elnathan the son of Achobor, and Gamarias the son of Saphan, and Sedecias the son of Hananias, and all the princes.   And Micheas told them all the words that he had heard when Baruch read out of the volume in the hearing of the people.'

[1] I must add that this is sheer guessing, because I have not studied what plans there are—*if* there are any—of the Temple's reconstruction.   Our Lord spoke in the treasury of the Temple, but we must remember that this was in another Temple altogether—the Temple built by Herod.

The story is becoming remarkably graphic; it gives us also a pleasant picture of cabinet life in the seventh century B.C. Micheas was so stirred by the reading of the Prophecy that he felt he must do something at once. He knew that his father was on the side of Jeremias and that if anything was to be done it must be done now. Unfortunately there happened to be a council going on down at the palace—the Temple was on the top of Mount Moriah, the palace was on the slope—and by the time his father, Gamarias, could be expected home the people would have dispersed and the spell would have been broken. The thing to do was to interrupt the meeting . . . after all, he knew everyone present and was related to half of them . . . the king was not there and nobody would mind much. So the young man knocked and went in.[1]

> 'Therefore all the princes sent Judi the son of Nathanias, the son of Selemias, the son of Chusi, to Baruch, saying: Take in thy hand the volume which thou hast read in the hearing of the people and come. So Baruch took the volume in his hand and came to them. And they said to him: Sit down and read these things in our hearing. And Baruch read in their hearing. And when they had heard all the words, they looked upon one another with astonishment; and they said to Baruch: We must tell the king all these words.'

There is no mistaking the source from which this part of the Prophecy is derived: for the narrative to be

[1]The only other familiar name in the assembled council is Elnathan, who had been sent to Egypt for the arrest of Urias. The Hananias mentioned as being the father of Sedecias may quite well be the false prophet whom Jeremias will have occasion to attack in the next reign.

as vivid as this we need an eye-witness—Baruch is the man. In spite of the genealogy to which Judi is treated, we do not know any more of him than what is given in the text; he will come into the story again, but only—as he does here—in the capacity of a messenger. It looks as though the plan which we have attributed to Micheas of getting something done while the people were still attending the ceremonies in the Temple was abandoned in favour of a second reading of the volume which had caused such a stir; and this time the reading would be *in camera*. We should notice the deference with which Baruch was treated when he arrived: he was asked to sit down. The noblemen had nothing against this scribe, who had probably been at school with most of them and who represented a prophet whom they had learned to respect. If the king had been there it would have been different, but with Joachim out of the way there was no harm in being civil to the opposition. So Baruch read his manuscript and the princes 'looked upon one another with astonishment'—as well they might. Jeremias had not spared his public in his sermons, and we may be sure that he left little out when he had these sermons written down. 'We must tell the king,' said the princes.

> 'And they [the princes] asked him [Baruch] saying: Tell us how thou didst write all these words from his mouth. And Baruch said to them: With his mouth he pronounced all these words as if he were reading to me, and I wrote in a volume with ink.'

There is something deliciously home-spun about the brave and faithful Baruch. He answered plainly what he thought was a plain question. But was it such a plain question? It seems highly unlikely that the princes should be lost in admiration—as Baruch evidently thought they were—at the secretary's skill in taking a dictation; it seems far more likely that they wanted to know how far Jeremias was involved in the affair and whether others had assisted in drawing up the document. These were things the king would want to know when the matter was put before him. If Baruch had taken down Jeremias's words as, over a course of years, the sermons had been delivered, then there was nothing to show that the prophet was still in the neighbourhood—he might, for all the princes knew, have followed Urias into Egypt—while if, on the other hand, Baruch had taken down the prophet's sermons in a solid block and quite recently, then presumably he was in hiding fairly near. Hence, 'Tell us how thou didst write all these words from his mouth.' We can imagine Gamarias feeling most uncomfortable when this question was put to Baruch by one of his colleagues: he, Gamarias, knew perfectly well how Baruch had written all these words, and he knew perfectly well also why the question had been put. He knew perfectly well also that Jeremias was staying in his father's house. Baruch's ingenuous reply about pronouncing with the mouth and writing with ink must have exasperated Gamarias.

> 'And the princes said to Baruch: Go and hide thee, both thou and Jeremias, and let no man know where you are.'

Gamarias breathes again! So the princes are taking a reasonable view of the situation: Baruch is being told unofficially to go and tell Jeremias, wherever he is, on no account to disclose his hiding place . . . and let Baruch, too, be careful not to show his face in Jerusalem.

> 'And they went into the king in the court, but they laid up the volume in the chamber of Elisama the scribe. And they told all the words in the hearing of the king. And the king sent Judi that he should take the volume, who, bringing it out of the chamber of Elisama the scribe, read it in the hearing of the king and of all the princes that stood about the king.'

Nobody could have complained that the manuscript was not doing full service: this was the fourth reading. One hopes that Jeremias was kept informed of all this. Now comes the climax of the story:

> 'Now the king sat in the winter-house in the ninth month, and there was a hearth before him full of burning coals. And when Judi had read three or four pages, he [the king] cut it with a penknife, and he cast it into the fire that was upon the hearth till all the volume was consumed with the fire that was upon the hearth. And the king and all the servants that heard these words were not afraid, nor did they rend their garments. But yet Elnathan and Dalaias and Gamarias spoke to the king not to burn the book, and he heard them not.'

The passage fixes the time of the year: the ninth month corresponds to November and December. Palestine can be exceedingly cold just then, and we are not surprised to find Joachim with a fire in his

room. In the East, books were written in three or four
parallel columns upon a roll; so it seems that each time
Judi got to the end of a column, Joachim, slashing at
the offending document, cut away what had just been
read and threw it into the blaze. Though the man was
in a vile temper and though there is nothing to be said
for his conduct, the action does suggest a certain dash
which it is gratifying to find in one whose dealings seem
for the most part to have been thoroughly underhand.
The courtiers were probably too stupefied to protest
against the burning; it is satisfactory to know, however,
that some of those present *did* venture a mild criticism.

> 'And the king commanded Jeremiel the son of
> Amelech, and Saraias the son of Ezriel, and
> Selemias the son of Abdiel to take up Baruch the
> scribe and Jeremias the prophet, but the Lord
> hid them.'

We are glad that no prince of Joachim's court was
heard to speak of what Baruch's naïve reply had led
them to suspect. The Lord—and, one ventures to
suggest, the Saphan family—hid the two men of God
successfully. But the incident was not over yet.

> 'And the word of the Lord came to Jeremias the
> prophet after that the king had burnt the volume,
> saying: Take ye again another volume, and write
> in it all the former words that were in the first
> volume . . . and Jeremias took another volume and
> gave it to Baruch the son of Nerias the scribe,
> who wrote in it from the mouth of Jeremias all the
> words of the book which Joachim the king of
> Juda had burnt with fire. And there were added
> besides many more words than had been before.'

Poor Baruch! Did his heart sink when he learned what the Lord had commanded his master? Or was he —on the showing of what we have already noted—so pleased with his penmanship that this new task came to him as an added chance of self-expression? In any case, he wrote the whole thing out again—and at greater length. ('The funny part of it was,' we can hear the aged Baruch telling his grandchildren years later, 'he kept on remembering things . . . so, of course, I wrote them in the book just as the words came from his mouth . . . in ink, you know.')

When St Teresa's manuscript was burnt by the devil it was restored to her miraculously; when the work of one human being is burnt by another human being the restoration has presumably to be effected by human means. It is as well that Jeremias had such means at his disposal; we have much for which to thank the brave and faithful Baruch.

So we close this section with a picture in our minds of Jeremias and Baruch in hiding. The two of them are hard at work on a revised text. When the brave and faithful Baruch is employed in proof correcting, Jeremias is busy with his thoughts and prayers. The major prophet is contrasting the characters of a father and son. Where Josias, at the reading of the word of God, had rent his garments, Joachim, at the reading of God's later message, had rent the word itself. Where the covenant, in the father's reign, had been offered to the Jews, the Prophecy, in the son's, had been committed to the flames. But just as Deuteronomy had risen in the first instance from the clouds of obscurity, so the Prophecy in the last had, like another Phœnix, risen from the smoke and ashes of Joachim's hearth.

To Josias and to Joachim came violent deaths, but where the father was mourned as having 'none like unto him before or after',[1] the son was to be 'cast out to the heat by day and the frost by night.'[2]

> 'And the rest of the acts of Joachim and the abominations which he wrought, are they not written in the book of the words of the days of the kings of Juda?'[3]

[1] 4 Kings xxiii, 25.   [2] xxxvi, 30.   [3] 4 Kings xxiv, 5; and 2 Paralipomenon xxxvi, 8.

CHAPTER XIII

KING JECHONIAS

HOLY SCRIPTURE is strangely silent about the latter part of Joachim's reign, so the preceding chapter must give place rather abruptly to the present one. All that may be said by way of prelude to the son's accession is that the father died in exile at Babylon. Joachim broke his oath of fealty to Nabuchodonosor, and the rising which he planned was a failure. Joachim passed out of Juda's history. Joachin (also called Jechonias) followed his father upon the throne at the age of eighteen, and showed by his three months of misrule that he intended to continue in the Joachaz-Joachim tradition. He reigned for ten days longer than his uncle had done and then surrendered to Nabuchodonosor. 'At the return of the year,' is Paralipomenon's contribution to the record of this reign, 'king Nabuchodonosor sent and brought him to Babylon, carrying away at the same time the most precious vessels of the house of the Lord. And he made Sedecias his uncle king over Juda and Jerusalem.'[1] The parallel passage in the Book of Kings[2] gives us far more information. It says how the young king, with his family and most of the aristocracy, went out to meet Nabuchodonosor, their deed of submission in their hands. It tells of the subsequent stripping of the Temple, and of the deportation to Babylon of all that was worth having in Jerusalem. Among the captives sent to

---

[1] 2 Paralipomenon xxxvi, 9ff.   [2] 4 Kings xxiv, 10-16.

Babylon on this occasion was the prophet Ezechiel. According to Jeremias[1] this convoy numbered 3,023 men, but the Book of Kings mentions the figure 10,000.[2] Curiously enough, Ezechiel, who must have got to know the king on the journey, even if he had not met him in Jerusalem before the surrender, has little to say about Joachin: he merely suggests that he was a somewhat ruthless 'lion' during his brief period of power, and adds that he was 'caged by the king of Babylon, that his voice should no more be heard upon the mountains of Israel'.[3] Possibly the fact that both men were exiles from their beloved Jerusalem had a softening effect upon their differences of outlook; certainly (if a fairly trustworthy tradition is to be believed) Joachin bore no ill-will towards Ezechiel, for he built a monument to the prophet's memory which is shown to this day in Chaldea.[4]

Joachin's subsequent career is interesting. He lingered on right through the heyday of Babylonian prosperity and outlived the man who had exiled him. After Nabuchodonosor's death he was released from prison by Nabuchodonosor's successor, Evil-Merodach, and was 'treated kindly'—even to the extent of being allowed some sort of little court of his own. This was in 560 B.C. He never saw Palestine again, in spite of what the false prophets had foretold.

What were Jeremias's movements during the three months of Joachin's rule in Jerusalem? We have no

---

[1] lii, 28.   [2] 4 Kings xxiv, 14.   [3] Ezechiel xix, 9.

[4] The tomb is near Birs Nimrod, the site of what was once Borsippa. It used to be a place of pilgrimage until the mausoleum fell into the hands of the Moslems. During the Middle Ages it was used as a library for Hebrew manuscripts. (See *The Story of The Bible* p. 579.)

means of finding out, but we may be pretty sure they were secret movements; if the prophet and his mission had been endangered in the previous reign they were just as much endangered in the present one. Jeremias refers once only to this miserable sovereign, and then in terms of some dislike:

> 'As I live, saith the Lord, if Jechonias the son of Joachim the king of Juda were a ring on My right hand I would pluck him thence. And I will give thee into the hand of them that seek thy life, and into the hand of them thou fearest, and into the hand of Nabuchodonosor the king of Babylon, and into the hand of the Chaldeans. And I will send thee and thy mother that bore thee into a strange country in which you were not born, and there thou shalt die . . . Is this man Jechonias an earthen and a broken vessel? Is he a vessel wherein is no pleasure? Why are they cast out, he and his seed, and are cast into a land which they know not? O earth, earth, hear the word of the Lord. Thus saith the Lord: Write this man barren, a man shall not prosper in his days: for there shall not be a man of his seed that shall sit upon the throne of David and have power any more in Juda.'

All of which was faithfully fulfilled. And this is all that we need say about Jechonias.

CHAPTER XIV

INCIDENTS IN SEDECIAS'S REIGN

i

WHEN Joachin had surrendered and had been removed, together with the cream of Juda's aristocracy, Nabuchodonosor presumably thought he need no longer worry about further defections; at all events, he allowed the Jews to nominate Joachin's successor. Matthanias was chosen. He was Joachin's uncle and another of Josias's sons. Nabuchodonosor changed his name to Sedecias, and it is by this name that we shall refer to him in the following pages. 'He reigned eleven years in Jerusalem, and he did evil before the Lord according to all that Joachim had done.'[1] It is possible that Sedecias had every intention of serving Nabuchodonosor, but that he was swept away on the wave of nationalist enthusiasm which characterised the early years of his reign. Elam's revolt against Babylon had encouraged Jerusalem in the belief that it might profitably attempt the same thing. The Jews saw in Joachin's deportation a sign that the Palestine remnant was being preserved by the Lord for a more general and a more successful rebellion than they had hitherto managed to engineer. In

---

[1] 4 Kings xxiv, 17-19. In fairness to Sedecias, however, it must be said that the chronicler of Kings is more severe than the prophet Jeremias about this sovereign. It is interesting to notice that in the Prophecy of Ezechiel Sedecias is nowhere referred to as 'king'; the Jews of the captivity regarded the exile Joachin as the only anointed king of Israel.

Sedecias's third year of rule we find the Jews making plans for a coalition which was to include Moab, Edom, Ammon, Tyre and Sidon; had this plan for a general revolt been favoured by Necho it might have been put into execution. But as it was, Egypt was still so spent after its defeat at Carchemesh that it was unwilling to commit itself. During these clandestine negotiations Sedecias thought fit to send a special embassy to Babylon assuring Nabuchodonosor of Juda's loyalty.[1] He may have meant it. But Juda was thirsting for war, and the king was dragged along a second time. By now Necho had died, and his successor, Psammeticus, was toying with the idea of another Palestine campaign. Juda prevailed upon its king to look into the chances of an Egyptian alliance. In 588 B.C. Hophra ascended the throne of the Pharaohs, and it was due to his enterprise that Sedecias decided to risk it. In that year the revolt was declared. This time Nabuchodonosor was not so patient or so trusting; he decided to destroy his vassal utterly. We shall see how he did this in the chapter which follows the present one.

'King Sedecias the son of Josias reigned instead of Jechonias the son of Joachim, whom Nabuchodonosor king of Babylon made king in the land of Juda. But neither he nor his servants nor the people of the land did obey the words of the Lord that He spoke by Jeremias the prophet. And king Sedecias sent Juchal the son of Selemias, and Sophonias the son of Maasias the priest to Jeremias the prophet, saying: Pray for us to the

[1] See Lods, *Prophets and The Rise of Judaism*, p. 48. The writer shows also that according to one text Sedecias may have gone to Babylon on this occasion himself.

I—j

Lord our God. Now Jeremias walked freely in the midst of the people, for they had not as yet cast him into prison.'

There are several things to notice about this passage. First it seems that as soon as Joachin (Jechonias as he is called here) was out of the way, it was intimated to the prophet that he could come out of hiding and go on with his work in the open. It would appear also that Sedecias, though 'not obeying the word of the Lord', had enough confidence in the minister of that word to ask his prayers when things were going badly in Jerusalem. Sedecias, as we have seen, was torn throughout his reign between Egypt and Babylon, between the voice of his people and the voice of his conscience. He was a shallow man, and no sooner had he made a decision than he unmade it. And when he found himself unable to make decisions on his own account he found himself unwilling to make them on God's account . . . 'he did not obey the word of the Lord'. But he wanted to know what *was* the word of the Lord; and this is perhaps something in his favour. So he sent a message about it to Jeremias by the hand of Juchal and Sophonias. These were two men who had shown themselves bitterly opposed to Jeremias's views: Juchal was to press for the prophet's death in a few months' time, and Sophonias was to share the fate of Phassur, whom Jeremias had cursed in Joachim's reign and with whom he was associated in the Temple. The prophet's reply to the king's request was not an encouraging one:

'Thus saith the Lord, the God of Israel: I will turn back the weapons of war that are in your hands, and with which you fight against the king of Babylon. . . I Myself will fight against you with an outstretched hand, and with a strong arm . . . and I will strike this city . . . I will give Sedecias the king of Juda, and all his servants, and all his people.'[1]

Jeremias went on from this to tell the king not on any account to listen to the false prophets who were urging him to look for a solution in an Egyptian alliance. 'Bend down your necks under the yoke of Babylon and serve him, and you shall live,'[2] was the prophet's advice to Sedecias, and he showed his sovereign the yoke which, at the Lord's command, he had been wearing as an instrument of penance and a symbol of Juda's slavery. (We shall deal further with this yoke in a moment.)

The strong line taken by Jeremias in his answer seems to have impressed the king; at all events he thought it worth while to send a few members of his court on a diplomatic mission to Babylon, and to allow these legates to take with them letters from Jeremias urging the exiles to stay where they were and not to look for a speedy return to Palestine. Among the noblemen whom Sedecias chose for this embassy were Elasa[3] the son of Saphan, and Gamarias the son of Helcias, both of them men with strong anti-Egyptian views; they were also, of course, as we remember from previous chapters, loyal supporters of Jeremias. These letters from the prophet contained much violent

---

[1] xxi, 4-7.   [2] xxvii, 12.

[3] Elasa was therefore the brother of Ahicam, who had seen to it in the previous reign that Jeremias was not suffered to go the way of Urias. (See xxvi, 24.) The Gamarias mentioned here is, of course, not the Gamarias of the 'treasury' incident.

matter directed against false prophets: it seems that
lying hopes were held out to every class of Jew at this
time—to the king, to the exile, to the vacillating
citizen—and that they were eagerly seized upon. One
of these lying prophets was Semeias the Nehelamite,
who, finding himself heavily censured by Jeremias,
wrote from Babylon to his friend Sophonias in Jerusalem, urging that Jeremias should be silenced as a
lunatic. The prophet got to hear of this, and there
followed a brisk interchange of correspondence between
the two capitals. This twenty-ninth chapter closes on a
very personal note indeed. Jeremias has, fortunately,
the last word: he predicts that Semeias will die child-
less and that none of his lying prophecies will bear
fruit. Both men's letters, printed in the twenty-ninth
chapter, are vitriolic.

ii

Again in connexion with a false prophet, an event
took place about two years later—in 593, therefore—
which it would be wrong for a biographer to leave out
but which most biographers must feel tempted to gloss
over. It is the curious affair of Hananias.

> 'It came to pass that Hananias the son of Azur,
> a prophet of Gabaon, spoke to me [Jeremias] in
> the house of the Lord, before the priests and all
> the people, saying: Thus saith the Lord of hosts,
> the God of Israel: I have broken the yoke of the
> king of Babylon.'

He then foretold what the other false prophets had
been foretelling with much insistence: namely, that

Joachin would return to the throne and that Juda would
be free for ever from the yoke of Babylon. Now, this
Hananias was of authentic prophetical and priestly
stock: Gabaon could show the same credentials as
Anathoth. It was simply a case of one prophet's word
against another's; both men employed even the same
formula in announcing their messages—'Thus saith
the Lord of hosts the God of Israel'. Hananias's
message, as all the priests and people would have been
perfectly aware, was in flat contradiction to Jeremias's
message.[1]

> 'And Jeremias the prophet said: Amen, the
> Lord do so; the Lord perform thy words . . . never-
> theless, hear this word which I speak in thy ears
> and in the ears of all the people: The prophets that
> have been before me and before thee from the
> beginning, and have prophesied concerning many
> countries and concerning great kingdoms, and
> of war and of evil and of pestilence . . . when the
> word shall come to pass *then* shall the prophet be
> known.'

Jeremias's method of meeting the situation is felt
to be slightly disappointing, but, after all, there was
nothing else he could do. Hananias had shown opti-
mism; he, Jeremias, had shown pessimism. Very
well, there was nothing left but to await the vindication at the bar of time . . . but remember (is the implication of Jeremias's words) that the *true* prophets of
the Lord have mostly predicted dooms.

> 'And Hananias the prophet took the chain from
> the neck from Jeremias the prophet, and broke it.'

[1] xxi, 26.

Notice that Jeremias still calls his opponent a 'pro-phet'. It must have been an exciting contest to watch: the two prophets, obviously very angry indeed, actually coming to the point of laying hands on each other. Hananias knew—as the priests and people knew —that the 'chain' or yoke which hung on Jeremias's neck was intended to signify the God-imposed sub-jection of Juda to Babylon. He deliberately went up to Jeremias and broke it. But Jeremias was not to be beaten by this.

> 'Thus saith the Lord: Thou hast broken chains of wood [said Jeremias] and thou shalt make for them chains of iron.'

By merely breaking a halter you cannot change the course of history; in fact, you are making things worse for yourselves by resisting this yoke of mine—you will be made to wear an iron one instead of this which is made of wood.[1]

There is a grim sequel to the event. It is this which one wishes one could gloss over; it is the third of the prophet's curses against individual opponents.

> 'And Jeremias the prophet said to Hananias the prophet: Hear now, Hananias, the Lord hath not sent thee, and thou hast made this people trust in a lie . . . this year thou shalt die, for thou hast spoken against the Lord. And Hananias died in that year in the seventh month.'

[1] Jeremias originally made six of these 'yokes'; one he kept for himself and the others he sent, at the Lord's command, to the kings of Edom, Moab, Ammon, Tyre and Sidon (xxvii, 3), who were to learn the same lesson. The yoke was evidently a simple construc-tion of wooden shoulder-pieces lashed together by bits of rope. It is believed that Jeremias wore this yoke for some three years; there is some doubt as to whether he began the use of the yoke in Joachim's or Sedecias's reign.

These repeated differences with members of the established clerical body might not have had such a damaging effect upon Jeremias's prestige, had not the issue of his quarrels invariably turned on the one thing —submission to the hated Babylon. How long Jeremias was permitted to walk at large after the accession of Sedecias we do not know, but it seems fairly certain that as the often-predicted fall of Jerusalem drew nearer Jeremias spent more of his time in prison; there are frequent references to his being 'shut up' during Sedecias's reign, which shows that the anti-Babylon feeling increased in proportion as Babylonian territory approached the territory of Juda. By the year 587 B.C. (which is the date of the incident we are about to examine), the siege had begun; Jeremias was still preaching his gospel of submission and fore-telling the destruction of the Holy City.

'The word of the Lord that came to Jeremias in the tenth year of Sedecias king of Juda, the same is the eighteenth year of Nabuchodonosor. At that time the army of the king of Babylon besieged Jerusalem, and Jeremias the prophet was shut up in the court of the prison which was in the house of the king of Juda. For Sedecias king of Juda had shut him up, saying: Why dost thou prophesy saying: Thus saith the Lord: Behold I will give this city into the hand of Babylon, and he shall take it?'

Sedecias had said a lot more to Jeremias in the same strain, complaining that his prophecies never seemed to favour his, the king's, declared policy. Could not the prophet reveal a single hope? Must it be *always* 'This city shall be destroyed, this city shall be destroyed'? The Lord Himself provided the answer to Sedecias's questions—and that in a rather unexpected way. The text suddenly leaves Sedecias altogether and takes up what seems to be a completely irrelevant account of Jeremias's financial transactions.

> 'The word of the Lord came to me, saying: Behold, Hanameel the son of Sellum thy cousin shall come to thee, saying: Buy thee my field which is in Anathoth, for it is thy right to buy it, being next of kin. And Hanameel my uncle's son came to me according to the word of the Lord to the entry of the prison, and said to me: Buy my field, etc. . . . and I understood that this was the word of the Lord. And I bought the field . . . '

Whereupon follow details of the contract: how it was sealed and signed when the money was weighed out, how Baruch was called upon to witness the legality of the transaction, and how the deed was finally put away in an earthen vessel 'that these writings may continue many days'. What, we ask, is the connexion? The explanation comes later on in the same chapter. 'To show you,' was roughly the line which Jeremias was told to take with the king, 'that I am *not* entirely hopeless as regards the future of our nation, I have just been negotiating for the purchase of a property which is at the present moment in enemy country. I am so firmly confident that Israel will one day be restored that to have closed with my cousin's offer must be regarded as both a sign and a prophecy. Yield therefore to Babylon, and you will find your country given back to you; resist, and you will find your country, though given back to you eventually, wasted and depopulated.'

As far as Juda and its king were concerned the result of this gesture of confidence on Jeremias's part was negligible. There was no move whatever towards surrender to Babylon. The episode had one good effect, however, in that it softened to some extent the anti-Jeremias feeling; he was regarded for the time being (until his next outbreak) as not quite so grievous a traitor as hitherto, and his prison regulations were somewhat relaxed. We shall have occasion to observe this fact in the incident now to be recorded. Otherwise the only person who benefited by the affair was Hanameel the son of Sellum, who got a cool seventeen shekels for a piece of land which he was unable to occupy. If Hanameel was at all typical of his race he must, as he walked away from his visit to the prison gate, a copy of the deed in one hand and a full purse in the other, have felt very pleased with himself indeed. One wonders if Jeremias, peering through iron bars at the retreating figure of his cousin, saw what perhaps he had not seen for a long time—a joke.

iv

'And the army of Pharaoh came out of Egypt, and the Chaldeans that besieged Jerusalem, hearing these tidings, departed from Jerusalem. And the word of the Lord came to Jeremias the prophet, saying: Thus shalt thou say to the king of Juda: Behold, the army of Pharaoh which is

come forth to help you shall return to their own
land into Egypt, and the Chaldeans shall come
again and shall fight against this city and shall
take it and shall burn it with fire.'

The siege of Jerusalem, as has been said, began in
587 B.C. Later in the same year—the siege started in
January—two things happened which complicated the
issue: the first was the arrival of Hophra's forces from
the south, the second was the famine which wore down
the besieged. The present story concerns the first-
named factor. The unexpected removal of Babylonian
troops inspired in the city a hope that Nabuchodonosor had fled before the face of the relieving Egyptians.
A lull in activities was the signal for increased propaganda on the part of pro-Egyptian militarists; it
was this wave of misplaced confidence which occasioned the further protests and prophecies on the part
of Jeremias. The sense of relief within the city was
destined to be short-lived: Nabuchodonosor had withdrawn only in order to concentrate on the Egyptians,
and, as soon as Hophra had been beaten back, the
siege was resumed as before.[1]

'Now when the army of the Chaldeans was gone
away from Jerusalem because of the Egyptians,

[1] It is thought that Nabuchodonosor did not actually engage with
Egypt on this occasion, and that Hophra was bribed to go away.
This is quite in the Egytian tradition of those times, but one somehow feels that Hophra was made of better stuff. He is the man who
(according to Herodotus) made war on the Sidonians, fought a naval
battle against the Tyrians, and forced the Ammonians to join his anti-
Babylonian confederacy. One feels he would, having come so far
for his campaign, have risked a battle with Nabuchodonosor and not
allowed himself to be bought off with Chaldean gold. There is a
mural tablet in the British Museum which shows an attractive
Hophra offering worship to his god. His career as Pharaoh ended
with deposition in 569 B.C., when he was succeeded by Amasis.

Jeremias went forth out of Jerusalem to go into the land of Benjamin, and to divide a possession there in the presence of the citizens.'

Jeremias then, availing himself of the temporary cessation of hostilities and finding that the prison restrictions had been relaxed in his favour on account of the good impression which his recent purchase had effected, decided to visit some friends of his who wanted a legal question settled. Many citizens were taking the chance of leaving what had been their prison yard for some months, and for Jeremias to attempt the harmless sortie along with the rest was not a matter which should have caused excitement. But it did.

'And when he was come to the gate of Benjamin, the captain of the gate who was there in his turn was one named Jerias the son of Selemias, and he took hold of Jeremias the prophet, saying: Thou art fleeing to the Chaldeans. And Jeremias answered: It is not so, I am not fleeing to the Chaldeans. But he hearkened not to him. So Jerias took Jeremias and brought him to the princes.'

One can hardly condemn the official. Jeremias was a marked man in Jerusalem and that he should be making off in a northerly direction was good enough evidence for an arrest. It was unfortunate that the gate of Benjamin happened to face the direction in which a deserter would flee, and it was unfortunate that Jerias should have been one of those who remembered the prophet's pro-Babylonian bias. There was nothing for it, Jeremias must be brought before the princes.

'The princes were angry with Jeremias, and they beat him and cast him into the prison that was in the house of Jonathan the scribe, for he was chief over the prison. So Jeremias went into the house of the prison and into the dungeon. And Jeremias remained there many days.'

A different lot of princes, evidently, from those who had twice shown consideration to the prophet in Joachim's reign. The punishment of beating seems monstrously unfair. Did the friends whom Jeremias had intended to visit decide their problem without the prophet's help? We do not know. Certainly they were kept waiting. We are inclined to wonder why Jeremias did not refer the princes to these 'citizens' in whose presence he was to have divided the possession. Perhaps he did speak about it to the princes, and perhaps they, only too glad of a chance of locking up so dangerous a character, refused to listen. The story is not finished.

'Then king Sedecias sending, took him and asked him secretly in his house and said: Is there, thinkest thou, any word from the Lord? And Jeremias said: There is. And he said: Thou shalt be delivered into the hands of the king of Babylon."

This gives us a picture which is characteristic of both men. Sedecias has heard of the prophet's arrest and subsequent confinement. He believes in the prophet's sincerity, but has not the courage to demand his release; he believes in the word of God, but has not the courage to profess it openly. And then Jeremias: as he had answered the official shortly at the gate, so he answers the sovereign shortly in the palace. Repeated imprisonments have made him a man of few words. He resents being made use of, when his public prophecies have been despised, as a household oracle. The picture of the interview suggests a solemn, tired, disappointed, exceedingly dignified prophet as contrasted with a fidgety, eager, hopeful, unkingly king. 'Is there,' says Sedecias with a nervous gesture, 'anything from God, do you think, which might throw a new light on this Babylonian affair? Any word, I mean, from . . . er . . . from the Lord?' 'Yes,' says Jeremias, 'there is.' And he tells the king he will be delivered into Babylon's power.

In a way we are sorry for Sedecias; he is so obviously an unsatisfactory specimen. All commentators take this opportunity of pointing out the king's fatal weakness of character. He is spoken of as the 'victim of his environment', he is described as having been 'moulded by the circumstances of his reign', he is dismissed as one who was 'invariably overruled by stronger wills than his'. My complaint is not that commentators borrow each other's facts—I do it myself— it is that they borrow each other's fancies and each other's formulæ. Because it is sheer fancy to say of Sedecias (or of anyone else for that matter) that he was powerless to resist the evil conditions in which Providence had allowed him to be placed. No man is *moulded* by circumstances, he is merely knocked about by them. No man is the *victim* of environment, he is merely the centre of it. A man who accepts God's grace makes his own character; a man who misuses God's grace spoils it. We may be weak or we may be strong, but the way we *develop* depends upon ourselves. Outward things have not of themselves the power to make us either lose or save our souls. 'There is nothing from without a man that entering into him can defile a man; but the things which come from a man, those are they that defile a man.'[1] Neither people nor books nor studies nor surroundings can do more than influence us. 'Neither height, nor might, nor any other thing can separate me from the love of Christ.'[2] '*Anima mea in manibus meis semper*,' sings the Psalmist: 'My soul is in my hands always,'[3] to do with it what I, independent of everyone else in the world, will.

When Jeremias had finished telling Sedecias what would happen to him he asked if the privations of his captivity in Jonathan's dungeon could be looked into and mitigated. Sedecias promised to do this, and Jeremias was 'committed into the entry of the prison'. Here Jeremias remained, fettered and manacled, for almost the rest of the siege. In addition to the change from cell to open porch Sedecias gave orders that the prophet's daily provision of food should be added to. 'A daily piece of bread beside broth till all the bread in the city were [i.e. should be] spent.' Which shows, incidentally, that the authorities were not entirely confident of Babylon's withdrawal.

v

From his place 'in the entry of the prison' Jeremias would have found it easier to carry on his ministry. So eager, in fact, does he seem to have been to preach his doctrine of submission that a deputation (consisting of people we have met before in this story) came to the king and told him that if this sort of thing went on

---

[1] cf. Mark vii, 14-23.   [2] cf. Romans viii, 39.   [3] Psalm cxviii, 109.

for much longer there would be wholesale desertions.
It was in the interests of the nation that this agitator
should be put under closer constraint—whatever the
king's personal feelings in the matter. The form of
Phassur's and Juchal's request is revealing:

> 'On purpose this man weakeneth the hands of
> the men of war that remain in this city, and the
> hands of the people, speaking to them according
> to these words. For this man seeketh not peace
> to this people but evil.'

Reading between the lines, it looks as though there
were not as many 'men of war' left in Jerusalem as there
should have been. By this time the famine had started
to ravage the city, and by this time also the Babylonian armies had returned to carry on the siege. No
wonder the princes were exasperated and apprehensive.

'And king Sedecias said: Behold, he is in your hand.'
Which is just what we would have expected him to say.
And he added: 'For it is not lawful for the king to deny
you anything.' What a sad summing up of Juda's
governmental system! The following account of what
the princes did to Jeremias is a complete story in itself,
perfect in its economy of words; it will need little
commenting upon.

> 'Then they took Jeremias and they cast him
> into the dungeon of Melchias the son of Amelech,
> which was in the entry of the prison; and they
> let down Jeremias by ropes into the dungeon
> wherein there was no water, but mire.'

Melchias, to whom this foul place belonged, was the
brother of Jeremiel, who, some twelve years previously,

had been sent by Joachim to find Jeremias and Baruch. The two sons of Amalech must have congratulated each other: they had got Jeremias at last, and Baruch would not now be difficult to catch. The details of the dungeon scene are in keeping with other scenes in Holy Scripture: Joseph was let down into a cistern; Daniel was let down into two separate dens; and both these men were rescued—as was Jeremias himself—under unusual circumstances. Though the text does not mention it, there must have been an interval of time between the last quoted passage and what follows.

> 'Now Abdemelech the Ethiopian, an eunuch that was in the king's house, heard that they had put Jeremias in the dungeon. But the king was sitting in the gate of Benjamin. And Abdemelech spoke to the king, saying: My lord the king, these men have done evil in all that they have done against Jeremias the prophet, casting him in the dungeon to die there with hunger. For there is no more bread in the city.'

It is strange that this foreigner, a black man and an unbeliever, should set about doing for Jeremias what no one of the prophet's own blood had thought of doing. Abdemelech's name must go down in history with those of the really noble souls who have responded to a grace of which they knew not the origin: Naaman in the Book of Kings, Darius in the Book of Daniel, the three Wise Men, the Centurion in the Gospel . . . and others. The lapse of time hinted at above is shown here by the fact that the city's bread supply, from being merely reduced, had run out. Abdemelech, then, realising that a prophet of Israel would soon die of starvation if nothing were done to prevent it, sought out the king, who was 'sitting in the gate of Benjamin'. Perhaps we have already conjured up a picture of Sedecias resting from his labours in the cool of the evening, and gazing out over his country from the porticoed front of Benjamin's gate. Perhaps we have thought of him as meditating, during this quiet hour, upon the mutability of human affairs, or upon the possibilities of next year's harvest, or upon the meal which he will be having at the palace in a little while, or upon his late father's trying ways. Perhaps we have already in the imagination coloured the scene with the setting sun—reddening the king's not very significant face; perhaps we have been listening to the rustle of silk as the evening breeze plays in the folds and fringes of the royal robe; perhaps, down the centuries, the perfume of the king's hair and beard has reached our nostrils. . . .

If such have been our thoughts and fancies, then we have been wide of the mark indeed. Sedecias was gazing out over a land which was not his but Babylon's: the enemy was encamped outside his walls. Benjamin's gate was barred and buttressed; Sedecias was 'sitting in it' because from that quarter, the north, Nabuchodonosor's attack would most likely be launched. The king may have been thinking of the abundance of next year's crops, but it is more probable that he was thinking of this year's lack of them. He was certainly not looking forward to his evening meal, because there was not going to *be* an evening meal. Nor would the sun have touched his countenance, because the gate of Benjamin did not face west. Sedecias was sitting in battle array and not in purple and ermine; his beard had not been attended to for weeks. He was intent upon one thing only: the siege. The preoccupation with which the king answered Abdemelech is, in this connexion, to be noted in the verses which follow in the text:

> 'Then the king commanded Abdemelech the Ethiopian saying: Take from hence thirty men with thee, and draw up Jeremias the prophet out of the dungeon before he die. So Abdemelech, taking the men with him, went to the king's house that was under the store house, and he took thence old rags and old rotten things, and he let them down by cords to Jeremias into the dungeon. And he said to Jeremias: Put these old rags and these rent and rotten things under thy arms and upon the cords. And Jeremias did so. And they drew up Jeremias with the cords, and brought him forth out of the dungeon. And Jeremias remained in the entry of the prison.'

There is this to be said for Sedecias, that he was as ready to be influenced by the worthy members of his council as he was by the unworthy. 'Very well, then,' might be a paraphrase of his curt reply to Abdeme-lech's request, 'take some men and do the thing yourself. If I stir a finger to release that man I shall be accused of being pro-Chaldean, and no one could say that about you—with all that Egyptian blood in you. (Ethiopia *is* more or less the same as Egypt, isn't it?) Anyway, do what you like about Jeremias, only don't bring me into it.' Left a free hand in the matter, Abdemelech rifled the palace lumber-rooms, and, carrying a bundle of cast-off clothing, made his way with

the thirty men to Jeremias's dungeon.[1]   The picture
of an Ethiopian nobleman leaning over the edge of
Jeremias's pit and dropping an armful of rags into the
void is a pleasing one.   And then, having told the
prophet what to do with the bits of material, Abdemelech hauls away at the rope and brings an emaciated
Jeremias to the surface.   One hopes that Jeremias was
not so worn out as to be incapable of celebrating his
release; one likes to think of the two men seated later
on in the same day at an embrasure in the prison entry
and drinking each other's health in what little water
was allowed them by their rations.   But even if for
one reason or another Abdemelech saw little of the
man he had rescued, he was to come in for honourable
mention on a later page of Jeremias's Prophecy.

vi

We have now got Jeremias again quartered in the
entry of Jerusalem's chief prison.   What the princes
thought of the transfer we do not know, but to judge
from the incident which lies immediately before us
they were not silent in their disapproval.

> 'King Sedecias sent and took Jeremias the
> prophet to him in the third gate that was in the
> house of the Lord.   And the king said to Jeremias:
> I will ask thee a thing, hide nothing from me.'

[1] Presumably the large number of the escort is due to the irregular
nature of the enterprise.   Had the king signed a deed of release there
would have been no need to defend himself against any action which
the princes might take to spoil Abdemelech's plans.   The point of
the rags of course was to prevent the rope cutting into the body,
which must have been sore after the treatment Jeremias had
received.

Sedecias, thoroughly apprehensive at the turn the siege was taking, again hoped to learn something which might unexpectedly alter the situation. Not daring, however, to compromise himself with his nobles by visiting the prison in person, he had Jeremias brought secretly to the Temple's third gate. According to Dr Streane, this was not a gate at all, but more probably a 'chamber retired from public observation and connected with a passage leading from the palace to the Temple'. In that case the spot was well chosen: near enough to the Temple for the prophet to be conveyed there without exciting much remark and far enough from the palace for the king to conduct his interview without fear of interruption.

'Then Jeremias said to Sedecias: If I will declare it to thee, wilt thou not put me to death? If I give thee counsel thou wilt not hearken to me. Then king Sedecias swore to Jeremias in private, saying: As the Lord liveth that made us, I will not put thee to death, nor will I deliver thee into the hands of these men that seek thy life.' (We should notice that Sedecias makes no promises about the prophet's second point—accepting counsel.) 'And Jeremias said to Sedecias: Thus saith the Lord of hosts, the God of Israel: If thou wilt take a resolution to go out to the princes of the king of Babylon thy soul shall live and this city shall not be burnt with fire . . . but if thou wilt not go out, this city shall be delivered into the hands of the Chaldeans, and they shall burn it with fire, and thou shalt not escape out of their hands.'

But Sedecias was unable to face the shame of it. Poor man, it was a ghastly predicament he was in: surrender to Babylon against what was still the policy of the realm . . . or fight it out against what was still the policy of the Lord. Even death and having to face God seemed better than life and having to face his friends.

> 'I am afraid,' [he confessed to Jeremias] 'because of the Jews that are fled over to the Chaldeans; lest I should be delivered into their hands and they should abuse me.'

If this was Sedecias's considered excuse, if this was *really* why he could not bring himself to take God's guidance for which he had asked, then it was a terrible admission. Not only was he afraid of the ministers who had urged him to trust in Egypt, but he was afraid of the masses *who had been afraid to trust in Egypt*. He dreaded his enemies, but he dreaded his friends far more. What would life hold for a man who had to listen to this in after years—'If you *had* to throw in your hand, why did you not do so earlier—with us— instead of allowing half the nation to perish in the siege?' I am afraid, said Sedecias, I am afraid. But dare we blame him?

'Let no man know these words,' was the king's command at the close of the interview which took place in the third gate that was in the house of the Lord, 'and thou shalt not die.' And he added, before they parted for the last time, a sadly characteristic instruction:

> 'If the princes shall hear that I have spoken with thee, and shall come and say to thee: Tell

us what thou hast said to the king and what the
king hath said to thee, thou shalt say to them:
I presented my supplication before the king that
he would not command me to be carried back to
the house of Jonathan to die there.'

Sedecias knew his princes. Sure enough they did find
out about the secret meeting, and they did come to
Jeremias in order to learn whatever might be learned.
But getting nothing out of Jeremias, they went, disappointed, away.

'And Jeremias remained in the entry of the
prison until the day that Jerusalem was taken.
And it came to pass that Jerusalem was taken.'

That '*was* taken' is, one feels, typical of the writer's
truly artistic way of accounting for the vindication of
his prophecies.

CHAPTER XV

THE FALL OF JERUSALEM

i

'And in the eleventh year of Sedecias, in the fourth month, the fifth day of the month, the city was opened, and all the princes of the king of Babylon came in and sat in the middle gate.'

SO READS the obituary notice of what was once Sion, the Holy City. That July day is one of the saddest in Jerusalem's sad history; it was commemorated later on by a yearly public fast. It had come at the end of an eighteen months' siege, a famine, disease, and a heat wave. Professor Cheyne's rendering of the occasion gives us a good idea of what must have taken place. 'There was still no thought of surrender,' he writes. 'Zedekiah stayed within the walls from pure weakness of mind; the "princes" because they would sooner starve than see their proud city laid low . . . the famished warriors could no longer defend the one weak spot in their fortifications. With a wild shout the besiegers poured in through a breach in the northern wall. It was night, and under cover of the darkness Zedekiah and his little army hurried in the opposite direction. By the rocky ravine of the Kedron they fled as far as the plains of Jericho; doubtless they hoped to cross the Jordan and elude their pursuers in the mountains of Moab. But it was too late; the Chaldeans were upon them. The army melted away; the king

was captured and carried to the headquarters at
Riblah, where, as a punishment for his perfidy, his
eyes were put out, his sons and "all the nobles of Juda"
having been previously executed.'[1]

Eloquent as this is, it is scarcely more telling than
the shorter account in the Prophecy:

> 'And when Sedecias the king of Juda and all
> the men of war saw them [the men of Babylon]
> they fled. And they went forth in the night out of
> the city by the way of the king's garden and by
> the gate that was between the two walls, and
> they went out to the desert.'

What drama there is in this single verse . . . almost—
but not quite—what melodrama. We can see a file
of muffled figures hugging the walls of the palace.
Then there is the stealthy cover-to-cover retreat in the
moonlight across the 'king's garden'. The more
exposed dash up the hill of Sion. The silent edging
through the little-used 'gate between the two walls' . . .
and the fugitives are out 'towards the way of the
desert.' . . .

Yes, it was an inglorious finish to an inglorious reign.
And Sedecias himself must have been bitterly aware
of this as he looked back on the city he had just left.
It was the city which his father had very nearly
rescued, the city which his two brothers had very nearly
wrecked; it was the city which he had tried to defend
and which he had now been obliged to yield into enemy
hands. He was leaving his city, his fathers' city, God's
city—by a back door.

If the king's objective was the eastern bank of the

[1] Op. cit. p. 167.

Jordan, he would have seen the first flames of Jerusalem's burning as he skirted the Mount of Olives. He would have smelled the smoke as it rolled after him up that ill-fated slope. From Olivet, again, he would have heard the cries of his people and the shouts of his enemies. Did he remember that by the same route David before him had fled from Jerusalem? Perhaps. But what he did not know was that Another of Juda's kings—the King of kings and Lord of lords—would one day tread the identical path. But this time it would not be in flight.

Near Jericho the royal party was taken. We picture the chase as finishing without much ceremony. A few minutes after the sound of horses' hoofs had been reported to the king there would have been the summary arrest. Sweating horses would have shied and stamped the ground; there would have been the rattle of harness as the men dismounted; there would have been the searching of faces until Sedecias's weak white face—whiter still in the moonlight, and drawn with anxiety and fear—would have been recognised by one of Nabuchodonosor's nobles; there would have been the reading out, in two languages, the warrant. And that would have been all.

The dawn sees Sedecias, escorted by Babylonian horsemen, being ridden in the direction of Rebla, where the Chaldean emperor has been quartered during the last sweltering months of his campaign against Jerusalem. A landscape which in daytime was tawny and flecked with shadows must have looked to the ex-king Sedecias, when he rode through it in the half-light of the very early morning, as grey and formless as his own soul.

'The king of Babylon slew the sons of Sedecias
in Rebla before his [Sedecias's] eyes.   He also
put out the eyes of Sedecias, and bound him with
fetters to be carried to Babylon.'

Sedecias is blind.   For the rest of his life he will
remember the last scene on which his eyes have rested—
the slaying of his sons.   Let us be generous.   If he has
deserved scorn he deserves sympathy just as much.

Weak or strong, changeable or consistent, there is
one thing which remains terribly constant and terribly
the same—death.   When most of what surrounds
human life is subject to alteration, when even the face
of nature can be modified from age to age, when night
can be virtually turned into day, there is still the fact
that a dead body looks the same now as it did when
Adam looked upon the dead face of his son Abel.   When
we see death at close quarters and suddenly—as
Sedecias saw it—we feel that the world has stopped in
the middle of its stride . . . and that there is not much
point in its going on.   Particularly when we see death
in the young, and the young whom we have loved (as
was the case with Sedecias), we feel that effort, educa-
tion, progress, activity of every kind, is meaningless.
'Why try any more,' we say, 'if the people we are doing
it for can go out—just like that?'   We are thrown off
our balance, and—such is the agony of grief—we have
no desire to regain that balance.   For most of us it is
not that we dispute God's right to take away our
friends, rather is it that we resent the demands which,
coming as they seem to do before their time, are made
by His superior love.   Obviously the author is entitled
to withdraw his works from circulation; it is only that

we feel it dreadfully when he presses his rights so far as to take the book out of our hands before we have read as far as we wanted.

Why is it that when we see the ordered run of life cut short we feel so bitter about ever having found a place in it ourselves? Why, moreover, are we shocked to find that life goes on in spite of the loss that has come to us? Perhaps the feeling that the world has stopped in mid-stride is not the strongest after all . . . the feeling that it has been heartless enough to go on—while *our* world has stopped—is even stronger.

What of the saints? They felt as deeply as we do, presumably, about the death of others. The difference must lie in the fact that while the saint *appreciates* the matter, we do not. Being unselfish in his affection, the saint can remember the theory of death; we—more earthly in our love—are blinded by the practice. The saint can 'rest content'; we, as suggested above, rest only in our misery. 'Leave me with my dead', we say; 'the temple is destroyed; let me sit among the ruins.'[1] The saint is less selfish. As after sin, so after sorrow; the saint picks up again the threads of life, while we delay.

True, we probably know well enough the answer to death, but unless we be saints, it fails to bring consolation at the time. 'Death reigned from Adam unto Moses,' explains St Paul; 'but not as the offence, so also the gift . . . they who receive grace shall reign in life, through Jesus Christ our Lord.'[2] Though small comfort to us perhaps—and no comfort at all to

[1] Which is only an echo, after all, of what Jeremias says himself: 'Rachel weeping for her children and refusing to be comforted' (xxxi, 15).

[2] Romans v, 14, 15, 17.

Sedecias, who never heard the words—it is, neverthe
less, true. Sedecias, when he saw the bodies of his two
boys lying on the sand in front of him, had nothing
to fall back upon in his pain; Jeremias, at the death
of Josias, had. Death—other people's—is always
frightful, but far less frightful must it be if we have
that to bring to it which a living faith provides.

ii

In August of the same year, 587, the walls of Jerusalem were pulled down, and eighty of the principal
men—priests as well as nobles—were slain. Nabuzardan, one of Nabuchodonosor's generals, left only
'some of the poor people that had nothing at all' in the
place that had once been Juda's capital. He had the
deserters from the siege sent into exile, he had the
Temple and the palace pillaged and destroyed.

And with that the history of Juda's kingcraft comes
to an end. It has not—unless we consider the reigns
of David, Ezechias and Josias—been a success. Israel's
constitution must undergo another drafting.

.   .   .   .   .

A sinister picture refuses to be brushed from the
mind. It is the picture of a twitching, aching, trussed-up
human form which is being jogged and bumped over
the two hundred and fifty miles which lie between
Jerusalem and Babylon. The human form is sweating
in the fierce heat of a Palestinian August. The head—
the only free member of that human form—is shaking
away the flies that tend to gather in the eyeless sockets.
Heavens, was it necessary to tie the man?

CHAPTER XVI

AFTERMATH

i

AFTER the evacuation of Hebrew-speaking people from Jerusalem and the consequent collapse of the kingdom of Juda as a local unit, a completely new phase is seen to begin in the history of the Chosen Race. Patriarchs and judges and kings have passed away; it was for Nabuchodonosor, at this stage an unbeliever, to recast the Jewish constitution and to provide for a workable system of government which was to obtain in Palestine during the early part of the period known as the Captivity. When Jerusalem fell, the Jews split up into three separate groups, each existing under widely different conditions. First, there were those who were deported to Babylon and who came to form one colony with those who had been exiled twelve years previously with Joachin (this first group was regarded as the flower of the nation—or, at all events, its fallen petals); next there were those who migrated to one or other of the less hostile neighbouring countries (this second group, because more scattered, disintegrated eventually; even the largest of these outposts, the Egyptian settlement, succumbed in time to pagan influences); and lastly, there were those who, rather than leave their native soil, remained in the hill country round about Jerusalem. It is this last group which is our present concern.

Living at first in caves and whatever shelter they could find, the remnant people were neither fugitives nor rebels. The life they led—until the little band was officially recognised by Nabuchodonosor—must have had about it something of the sad romance of both flight and outlawry. The need for some sort of leader very soon manifested itself, and Godolias the son of Ahicam was chosen. This is the first time we have come across Godolias, though his father and brother are familiar to us from earlier incidents connected with Jeremias: Ahicam was the man who had hidden Jeremias in Joachim's reign, and Gamarias was the courtier who had lent his treasury for the reading of the Prophecy by Baruch. Godolias was probably one of the few remaining members of Juda's aristocracy, and it was natural that the 'poorest in the land' should turn to him for protection. Retiring to an estate at Masphath, Godolias gathered round him all who cared to throw in their lot with the expatriated band, and soon the Jews who had sought refuge with neighbouring tribes began to trickle back to what was now becoming almost a rallying centre for the dispersed. Masphath (where Godolias lived, not as a prince or a general, but as a sort of rather domesticated Robin Hood) had been associated many centuries earlier with the judgeship of Samuel; Godolias, another Samuel, judged the people's causes from the place where Saul had been publicly proclaimed king.[1]   Samuel's tomb

---

[1] This is not to be confused with the city of the same name in Gilead. Samuel's Masphath is a village 2,930 feet above sea level, a few miles north-west of Jerusalem, in the land of Benjamin. Asa, king of Juda, had fortified it against attacks from the northern kingdom (3 Kings xv, 22), and it still had some of the advantages of a little garrison.

is reverenced there to this day, while Godolias's memory has been preserved only in the pages of the Prophecy.

> 'Now Nabuchodonosor king of Babylon had given charge to Nabuzardan the general concerning Jeremias, saying: Take him and set thy eyes upon him and do him no harm, but as he hath a mind to do, so do with him. Therefore Nabuzardan sent and took Jeremias out of the court of the prison, and committed him to Godolias the son of Ahicam, the son of Saphan, that he might go home and dwell among the people.'

This extract seems to show that Jeremias was known to Nabuchodonosor before the capture of Jerusalem; the Babylonian would hardly have given such express injunctions merely on the strength of a rumour which told of the prophet's anti-Egyptian sympathies. The passage seems to justify the belief that Jeremias did as a fact journey all the way to Babylon in Josias's reign and bury his girdle there at the Lord's command. The important part about this extract, however, is not the light it may or may not shed upon the happenings of Josias's reign, but the light which it actually does shed upon the formation of Godolias's colony at Masphath. It shows that Nabuchodonosor very soon saw the advisability of having at least a percentage of Jews in the neighbourhood of Jerusalem; they, better than the new-comers, would know how to cultivate the land to best advantage; they, better than the new-comers, would be able to keep up trade connexions which might otherwise lapse; they, better than the new-comers, would know the methods used by

neighbouring tribes in guerilla warfare.   Nabuchodonosor even allowed Godolias's company to practise
a certain amount of their religion.   Hence it was that
Jeremias could take his place at Masphath without the
slightest feeling that his work as a prophet would be
hindered by the officers of Babylon; Babylon, as he
had always said it would be, was far more tolerant of
the Jews' religion than had been expected.   In fact
it was far more tolerant of the Jews' religion than were
the Jews.

It is difficult for us—Catholics living in twentieth
century England—to visualise the conditions of that
peculiar exiled-but-still-at-home existence at Masphath.
In this century (much more than in the last) we have
come to enjoy, undisturbed, a Christianity which is so
organised, so well drilled, so recognisedly correct, so
universally accepted, so—I mean this in a compli-
mentary sense—'Martindaled', that a Church without
its own liturgy, hierarchy, press and art is almost
inconceivable.   But this is roughly what Godolias's
Jewish community was.   It would be as if the whole
Catholic population of England to-day were reduced
to an indiscriminate handful under the undefined
leadership of a 'scribe'—someone like Mr Arnold Lunn
—and confined to the limits of Hampstead Heath.   No
bishops, no societies, no bazaars, and only a few dis-
used army huts to serve as a metropolitan cathedral
(and with Fr Vincent McNabb as the one remaining
prophet in the land).   No, however strong our colours
and however living our models, we can scarcely paint a
picture of this curious little Jewish commonwealth of
the sixth century B.C.

ii

Just when we have got to the place in the text where we would expect Jeremias to tell us something about the kind of life he took up at Masphath we find ourselves whisked back again to the time of the prophet's imprisonment—the writer has forgotten something.

> 'But the word of the Lord came to Jeremias when he was yet shut up in the court of the prison, saying: Go and tell Abdemelech the Ethiopian, saying: Thus saith the Lord of hosts, the God of Israel: Behold, I will bring My words upon this city, and they shall be accomplished in thy sight and in thy day. But I will deliver thee in that day, and thou shalt not be delivered into the hands of those whom thou fearest . . . thy life shall be saved for thee because thou hast put thy trust in Me.'

It seems that Jeremias, in recording the rushed events of the last few months (changing the scene from Jerusalem to Rebla, from Rebla back again to Jerusalem, and from Jerusalem to Masphath), has somehow overlooked the sequel to the Abdemelech affair. Perhaps Baruch, writing many years later at the prophet's dictation, put down his pen at this point and called Jeremias's attention to the omission. 'Didn't you tell me once,' we can imagine the secretary saying, 'that there was some special revelation to do with the safety of that Ethiopian friend of yours? I think we ought to put it in if you can remember what it was; he did more than any of us to help you.' 'Of course, yes, how silly of me,' says the prophet, 'we can fit it in here. As long

L—j

as it's mentioned before the Godolias period it will be all right. Ready? Then write this: "When Jeremias was yet shut up in the court of the prison," ' etc.

We can further reconstruct the effect of this insertion upon the person whom it most concerned. Abdemelech is back again in his own country. He has quitted Jerusalem soon after the Babylonian occupation, and is now living in the memories of the court life which he had enjoyed under Sedecias, the last of Juda's kings. Faithful to his late masters, he reads the literature of Judaism whenever he gets the chance. At the moment a newly-issued edition of Jeremias's prophecies lies open on the old man's knee. He has heard rumours of Jeremias's presence here in Egypt, but somehow or other ... well, the dungeon interlude was a long time ago now, and the two men have drifted apart. Then the Ethiopian comes to the place in the text where his name is mentioned. A smile lights up his face. He reads on ... the fall ... Godolias ... then, unexpectedly, 'Go tell Abdemelech saying,' etc. He puts the volume on the table and decides to find out next day whether or not the prophet has come to Egypt after all. A gleaming row of teeth shine in the night of his Ethiopian skin, and the old gentleman, happy beyond words, goes up to bed.

The brave and faithful Baruch is to be congratulated for having reminded Jeremias of the omission.

iii

Jeremias, for all his austerity and outspokenness, must have possessed great charm. He made friends with Nabuzardan, the Babylonian general.

It seems that after Jeremias had been attached for about a month to the Godolias community he was invited to an interview with the general, who was getting ready to go back to Babylon.[1] The offer which the foreigner made to Jeremias on this occasion was a handsome one:

'If it please thee to come with me to Babylon, come; and I will set my eyes on thee [i.e. see that you will be all right]. But if it do not please thee to come with me to Babylon, stay here. Behold all the land is before thee; whither it shall please thee to go, thither go.'

The words of Jeremias's reply are not given, but he decided to go back to Godolias. 'And Nabuzardan gave him victuals and presents, and let him go.' We like to think of Nabuzardan, the hard-bitten general of numberless campaigns, going home disappointed at the prophet's refusal. Here is another witness to that quality in Jeremias, which seems to have attracted friends; Abdemelech and Nabuzardan were not only separated from him by faith, but were also men of different blood. A biographer of Jeremias should never be tired of insisting on this gift for making friends; it shows more clearly than anything else that the prophet was not a forbidding figure. If there was occasionally bitterness in Jeremias's soul, it was because of the sweetness that was unable to find expression. If he was hard upon the people he loved, it was only because he knew so well the meaning of love. If the

[1] It is possible that Jeremias had in any case to report himself every few weeks to the Chaldean authorities, and that Nabuzardan wished to assure himself that Nabuchodonosor's instructions were being carried out.

pages of his Prophecy are wet with tears, it is only because the same pages could have equally well proclaimed his laughter.

When we read of the prophet's decision we wonder perhaps what prompted it. Would he not have done infinitely better to have joined his countrymen in exile? The Babylonian Jews, and not the straggling Palestine colony, were the real representatives of the race—more in number, worthier in kind. Had he not himself compared the departed to good figs, and those that remained to bad? Why waste time and eloquence on a dull and dispirited minority when a more or less patriotic and intelligent majority awaited him in Chaldea?

I submit that Jeremias refused to go to Babylon because he knew it would be less pleasant to stay in Judea. Elsewhere I have suggested that for the same reason Daniel stayed in Chaldea when he might have returned to Jerusalem; elsewhere I hope to suggest that for the same reason Ezechiel stayed in Tel-Agib when he might have gone to Babylon. The theme is a favourite one with me. Let us see if, when applied to the case of Jeremias, there is any foundation for it.

Everything was in favour, naturally speaking, of accepting Nabuzardan's proposal. The general offered a peace and retirement which would have been out of the question at Masphath or anywhere else in Judea. Forty years of rejected ministry were telling on Jeremias, and he longed for a more tranquil apostolate; if there is one thing more exhausting than giving yourself out to an appreciative audience, it is giving yourself out to an unappreciative one. In Babylon, as Nabuzardan's (and possibly even Nabuchodonosor's) friend,

Jeremias would at last be able to rest; or if not to rest, at least to work among people who understood his mission. Again, it was the prophet's highest ambition to see his people purged of their idolatry; in Babylon, as he had been expressly told by the Lord, this would take place. He longed to witness this process and, in the rôle of guide, to further it. As a reformer he had signally failed, as a chaplain he might yet succeed. In Babylon, lastly, there would be Daniel and Ezechiel; he would be able to treat of the things that mattered most with men who thought as he did. Yes, everything pointed, naturally speaking, to Babylon as the scene of Jeremias's declining years.

Against this there would have been nothing to influence the prophet but the need of his rather scratch compatriots at home. Could the remnant dispense altogether with the services of a prophet? This was the question which Jeremias had to face. 'No,' he answered, 'I don't think it can.'

There was no command from God on the subject; there was no appeal on the part of the remnant for Jeremias's continued presence. Jeremias presumably prayed about the matter, and then decided to stop on. Did he remind himself of what the Lord had said to him long ago? 'Assuredly it will be well with thy remnant . . . assuredly I will help thee in the time of affliction.' This echo from Josias's reign was the sole expressed encouragement from the Lord to which Jeremias was able to turn. And that did not tell him very much.

'Jeremias dwelt in the midst of the people that were left.' Throwing away his chances? Wasting his powers? Evading his mission? One wonders. Would Christ

have said that because he was not 'realising himself'
he was therefore wasting himself? Our Lord seems
again and again to have withdrawn the sickle from His
own harvest just when we would have thought it was
necessary that He should reap. In the light of the
Gospel one hesitates to say of a man that he is evading
the responsibilities of his vocation when he is seen to
be throwing away the ladders of success. When Our
Lord as a boy 'went up to Jerusalem according to the
custom of the feast', he had it in his power—even on the
natural plane, entitled at the age of twelve to choose
his calling—to stay in Jerusalem and study at the
schools. What surer way of establishing a permanent
connexion with the Temple? With such a theological
training and with a long association with the Jerusalem
public to draw from, His Gospel—when He should
choose at the age of thirty to declare it, would inevitably
be listened to. But what, in fact, took place? Precisely
when the career seemed to open up its possibilities He
decided not to embark upon that career for another
eighteen years. He chose not to graduate as a scribe,
but to serve as a carpenter's apprentice. He Who
could have shone at Antioch, Alexandria, Rome,
Athens, decided not to shine at Nazareth instead.
He 'threw away His chances'; He 'wasted His powers';
He 'evaded His mission'. And He did so every bit
as deliberately as Jeremias did when the Masphath
decision was made. He did so every bit as deliberately
as when, from the pinnacle of the Temple, He refused
to take Jerusalem by storm . . . as when, from the
cross, He refused to come down in order to justify His
claims. It was not Christ's way to 'snatch' His Kingdom; He wanted to *win* His Kingdom for mankind.

And His way of winning it was to keep it at arm's
length, apparently, until the time was ripe.[1]   It is
only with the eye of faith that we can follow this
amazing principle of action.

It is faith which alone makes possible the burning of
boats, not after, but *before*, the stream is crossed. By
faith a man may not only uproot a mulberry-tree and
watch it being cast into the sea,[2] but he may do so when
he is sitting on the branches. By faith a man may not
only move mountains,[3] but he may move them back
again, and place them in the way of his progress. 'By
faith Abraham, when he was tried, offered Isaac':[4]
throwing away the one sole hope, you would have said,
of prophecy being verified. 'By faith Moses, when he
was grown up, denied himself to be the son of Pharaoh's
daughter':[5] throwing away the one sole hope, you
would have said, of setting his plans in motion. But
prophecy *was* verified, the plans of Moses *were* set
in motion. And if we want to know more about this
faith we can 'look upon Jesus, the author and finisher
of faith, Who, having joy set before him, endured the
cross, and now sitteth on the right hand of the throne
of God.'[6]

There is justification, then, for Jeremias's choice.
He, as Moses did, 'chose to be afflicted with the people
of God'[7] rather than be lulled into temporal security.
Temporal considerations weighed little with Jeremias.
People who look unafraid at the things of eternity can
afford to be casual about the things of time. Jeremias
was granted to see further into the secrets of eternity

[1] Luke v, 12-16; Mark iii, 12; John vi, 15.   [2] Luke xvii, 6.
[3] Mark xi, 23.   [4] Hebrews xi, 17.   [5] Ibid., 23.
[6] Ibid., xii, 2.   [7] Ibid., xi, 25.

than we are granted to see: he saw a dawn where we see night. Jeremias saw—as regards this world, let alone the next—a return from exile and the coming of a Saviour. He saw that God was in His heaven and that all would yet be well.

'They shall be My people, I will be their God.' Such was the vision of Jeremias. Magnificently alive is the prophet's hope; magnificently eloquent, in its simplicity, his song. There is no throwing away of chances in Jeremias, because he sees in Whose hand all the 'chances' of mankind are held.

iv

We have arrived at the point where Jeremias is lodged with Godolias and his band of dispossessed Jews. It is impossible to say how long this condition of things continued. Some commentators seem to think that the community broke up quite soon, whilst others give it five years. A reason for following the view which extends the period is that *some* time in the prophet's career should be left free for the possible composition of Lamentations, and this seems as probable a time as any. As suggested above, it is by no means certain that Jeremias wrote Lamentations; if he did, then the most suitable time for the composition would be now—when Jerusalem was in ruins. Allowing, then, that he did write the book and that he wrote it now, a reasonable amount of time must be given him in which to have done it.[1] Leaving the time question

[1] It is only fair to say that a number of authorities—even among those whom I have followed throughout this book and who have no doubts about the Jeremian authorship of Lamentations—hesitate to

open, we can say that at this period it was Jeremias's concern to nurse the sorely punished remnant in their hour of misery. To the children of promise Judea must have seemed a dismal night-nursery in a home which was destined for ever to be occupied by strangers. A story (as grisly as any in the nursery bookcase) must here be told: it is the story of one man's generosity and another's jealousy, it is a story of trust and treachery, of blood, brutality and revenge.

attribute the date of composition to so late a period in the prophet's life. They seem to think that Jeremias wrote the Book of Lamentations after the death of Josias, when Jerusalem was lying about him in moral rather than in actual ruins.

CHAPTER XVII

THE ISMAHEL SCANDAL

'And when all the captains of the army that were scattered through the countries, they and their companions, had heard that the king of Babylon had made Godolias governor of the country and that he had committed unto him the men and women and poor of the land, them that had not been carried away captive to Babylon, they came to Godolias at Masphath. And Ismahel the son of Nathanias, and Johanan and Jonathan the sons of Caree, and Sareas and the children of Ophi, and Jezonias the son of Maachati, they and their men . . . returned out of all the places to which they had fled, and they came into the land of Juda to Godolias. And they gathered wine and a very great harvest.'

THE LORD seems to have blessed the remnant with temporal prosperity: the crops were good and the government of Godolias was popular. The people were mostly a God-fearing and a hard-working lot, and, had not one of their number upset things by his ambition, anything might have happened. But the chances of healthy development were stifled:

'All the captains came to Godolias and said to him: Know that Baalis the king of the children of Ammon hath sent Ismahel the son of Nathanias to kill thee. And Godolias believed them not.'

were worth robbing that they suffered what the next
extract will record; it was simply that they were on
the direct route to the headquarters of Babylon's
occupation; and, since they had to pass through
Masphath on the way, Ismahel was for taking no
risks. Had the pilgrims been returning from Jerusalem
instead of going towards it, they would probably have
been left alone. Hitherto Ismahel has abused hospitality, now he touches something even more sacred
still—a religious procession.

> 'Ishmael the son of Nathanias went forth from
> Masphath to meet them, weeping all along as he
> went. And when he had met them he said: Come
> to Godolias the son of Ahicam.'

The pilgrims were indeed to go the way of Godolias
the son of Ahicam. Having managed to convince the
pilgrims of his sincerity he slew them and 'cast them
into the midst of the pit'. Ten men, however, he
spared; this was not because of any wave of mercy
which swept over his black heart, but simply because
he was given to understand that they had 'stores'
at home, of wheat and barley and oil and honey.
Ismahel's plans required, for their successful issue, a
considerable store of provisions, and this was a wind-
fall on which he could hardly have expected to count;
the gambler's luck was with him. The next step was to
carry off the remaining inhabitants of Masphath into
the desert. The plan in the madman's mind was to
establish a Hebrew colony in Ammon of those who
favoured his aims, methods and manners generally;
Baalis, king of Ammon, would have fallen in with this
scheme. But Ismahel's arrangements did not even-
tuate, because—

'Johanan the son of Caree, and all the captains of
the fighting men that were with him, heard of the
evil which Ismahel the son of Nathanias had
done, and, taking all the men, they went out to
fight against Ismahel the son of Nathanias. And
they found him by the great waters that are in
Gabaon. And when all the people that were with
Ismahel had seen Johanan the son of Caree and all
the fighting men that were with him they rejoiced.
And all the people whom Ismahel had taken went
back to Masphath. But Ismahel the son of
Nathanias fled with eight men from the face of
Johanan, and went to the children of Ammon.'

The story of abduction, pursuit, rescue and flight
reads like a desert romance—which, if you cut out the
introduction and epilogue, it was. As it stands, however, it is one of the most bloodstained pages in Scripture; the incident is positively dripping. It is surely
one of the evils of the present time that contempt for
human life is in some sort canonised. But to despise
life (or death) can never be a bravery born of lofty
indifference. Far from being something lofty, such an
indifference is one of the signs and fruits of paganism.
The Church may tell us to regard ourselves as dust,
but it never says we may consign ourselves to the
dust-bin. The Church may remind us that we are
merely ashes, but it does not wish us to be tossed into
the ash-tray.

The extract which has been quoted is so graphic that
we are almost certainly safe in believing Jeremias to
have been among 'the rest of the people that were at
Maphath', and was, therefore, one of those that rejoiced

when the gallant Johanan was seen riding up with his relieving force. One would like to have been present for this at the great waters that are in Gabaon. The rescue is worthy of the sound-screen. There is the dashing Johanan, clean-cut, bright-eyed, etc., galloping over the sands in a desperate effort to reach the retreating caravan this side of the Ammon border. With him, but slightly behind, ride the 'captains of the fighting men'. At Gabaon the two groups meet—Johanan has caught up after all. There are shouts from the captives, shouts from the men of Ismahel, shouts from the men of Johanan, shouts from everybody. Horses toss their manes in the air and prance about in the sun . . . glistening flanks are slapped by the flats of swords . . . harness and trappings make a brave accompaniment to the music of the skirmish . . . the dust of the desert flies up in clouds, blinding the fighters and the fought-for alike. And all the while there is the sound of falling water: one great pool is pouring itself (with a nice sense of background values) into the glittering basin of another.[1] Then one man is seen to extricate himself from the confusion . . . then another, and another . . . until eight figures, with Ismahel at their head, are found to have left the scene of the struggle: they are already swallowed up in the quivering haze of the horizon, bequeathing only the dishonoured name (to be whispered in terms of threat by reproving parents) of the man who was at once a prince and an assassin.

It has been suggested above that the romance of the story was disqualified by the sequel. The after-events

---

[1] 'There is still an ancient broken reservoir on the west side of the hill of Gibeon [our Gabaon], and in the wet season there is a considerable pond in the plain below the modern village. The modern village is called El-Jib.' (Binns, op. cit. p. 130.)

showed, unfortunately, that the hero Johanan was not
such a very satisfactory young man after all. Chivalrous enough in the clash of arms, Johanan was not the
man to persevere when the din of battle had died down.
There are many such swashbuckling footlight perso-
nalities, who readily defend a cause or a woman or an
ideal, but who are unwilling to defend the consequences
of their defence. Here is the rest of the story:

'Then Johanan the son of Caree and all the
captains of the men that were with him took the
people whom they had recovered from Ismahel,
and they departed and sat as sojourners in Chamaam which is near Bethlehem. [This they did]
in order to go forward and enter into Egypt from
the face of the Chaldeans, because they were
afraid of them, because Ismahel had slain Godolias
the son of Ahicam. And they said to Jeremias the
prophet: Let our supplication fall before thee, and
let the Lord show us the way by which we may
walk . . . . Now after ten days the word of the Lord
came to Jeremias, and he called Johanan and all
the captains and all the people from the least to
the greatest, and he said to them: Thus saith the
Lord the God of Israel: If you will be quiet and
remain in this land, I will build you up and not
pull you down. . . . Fear not because of the king
of Babylon of whom you are greatly afraid; fear
not, for I am with you to save you and to deliver
you. . . . And it came to pass that when Jeremias
had made an end of speaking all the words of the
Lord, Azarias the son of Osaias and Johanan the
son of Caree and all the proud men made answer

> to Jeremias, saying: Thou tellest a lie: the Lord
> our God hath not sent thee, saying: Go not into
> Egypt to dwell there.'

In the above quotation much of the text has been
left out; the whole passage deserves study—particularly the very long speech in which Jeremias, already
suspecting that his hearers have made up their minds,
irrespective of God's message to them, outlines the
evils which disobedience must involve. The prophet
makes the issue perfectly clear: safety in submission,
peril in flight. It is exactly the same issue which, all
his life, he has been begging the Jews to face.

The first resting-place after the movements of the
last few days was a spot which 'is near to Bethlehem'.
Its suitability lay in the fact that it was close to the
main caravan route to Egypt—a fact, incidentally,
which again shows that minds were made up before
the request was made for the guidance of God upon the
next step to be taken. Bethlehem: there is tragic
incongruity in the choice of this place before all others.
To us of the New Testament the very word breathes
peace; and here, in the Old Testament, we find it
threatening further bloodshed. The Bethlehem of our
dreams stands always for the beginnings of light and
life and hope and love; while here, in the Jeremias
story, we find it a halting place on the way to further
darkness, death, hopelessness and lack of love. The
Jews were fugitives 'fleeing from the face of the Chaldeans', and Bethlehem was the place from which they
began their flight. Perhaps there is no incongruity
after all: Christ, too, was a 'sojourner' in Bethlehem;
Christ, too, was an exile from the Holy City; Christ,

too, was soon to embark upon a flight into the land of
Egypt. Bethlehem, 'a little one among the thousands
of Juda',[1] has, in the course of its history, witnessed
great things.

So at the end of ten days, spent by Jeremias in what
was presumably some sort of retreat, it was announced
to the remnant what were the wishes of the Lord. Then,
having turned down the message, the people lost no
time in making a move; they 'went into Egypt and
they came as far as Taphnis'. What a fearful mortifi-
cation it must have been to Jeremias to see the whole of
his life's work thus contradicted! That he had been
accused of falsifying the word of God was bad enough,
but that he should have to watch preparations being
made for a voluntary exodus from the Holy Land on
the part of the few remaining Jews that had not been
forced to leave must have been galling indeed. And of
all places in the world—Egypt! The amazing part of it
is that Jeremias went with them.

Taphnis is about fifteen miles west of what is now the
Suez canal. Thus it was a journey of about two hundred miles from Bethlehem to Taphnis; how long it
took and what route was chosen for it we do not know.[2]
The travellers set out in October, and this is the sum
total of our information. Commentators are strangely

[1] Micheas v, 2.

[2] We like to think, however, that at least the latter part of the
journey was made over the ageless caravan road of which Mr
Morton writes in his book about Palestine, *In The Steps of The
Master*. 'It was along this road,' he says, 'that Joseph was led into
captivity. It was the road over which the first great Jewish financier,
Solomon, sent his sandalwood and his spices to the markets at
Memphis. It was a road that led everywhere: to Damascus in the
north, to the desert city of Petra in the east, to Egypt in the south
. . . I remembered again that this was the way Joseph and Mary fled
with a Child into Egypt.' (p. 3.)

reticent about this flight; legend is silent. Given a fast car, one might reach the eastern arm of the delta in about five hours from Bethlehem; given bad roads, a mixed assembly of travellers, inability to make much headway between the hours of eleven and two, and all the incidental difficulties of avoiding bedouin attacks, re-stocking with provisions, illnesses, etc., the time spent on the expedition may easily have amounted to four or five weeks.

And what, in the meantime, of those Jews who were still of the opinion that a sacred land overrun with heathens was better than a heathen land overrun with heathens? Did a yet smaller remnant stay on in Judea to face the consequences of the Ismahel disturbance? Certain it is that not all decided upon Egypt as a haven of safety, but apart from this there is little that can be said that is not sheer conjecture. 'The little group of Jews which had begun to gather round Gedaliah [Godolias] dispersed,' writes Professor Lods in the work already quoted; 'many took refuge in Egypt, where they swelled the ranks of the Judean settlers already established in the Delta, even going as far as Pathros, that is to say to Upper Egypt, the "land of the south" (*pa-tu-risi*). There were doubtless fresh disturbances in Palestine five years later, for Nebuzaradan, at that date (581), again deported 745 Jews. They were, however, only the despairing efforts of the last Israelite monarchy before its final extinction.'[1] With Jeremias and his companions we can now leave Palestine for good.

[1] *The Prophets and The Rise of Judaism*, p. 50.

CHAPTER XVIII

TOWARDS EGYPT AND EXILE

TWO thousand five hundred years is a longish time, but the flight of fancy once made, we should not find much difficulty in judging what were the thoughts of those who travelled from Palestine to Egypt in the hope of finding abroad what they had neglected to look for at home.

Imagining ourselves, then, to be among the Jewish crowd on this journey of self-imposed exile, we spend our time—when not either trotting ahead to see about a camping site or else lagging behind to pick up the stragglers—reflecting somewhat dismally upon the missed opportunities of the past and the mixed possibilities of the future.

Since our object is to get to Egypt as quickly as possible, we are cutting across country wherever the country allows of it. We are a large enough force to be tolerably safe from the brigands of the plain, and we have no desire to be seen upon the highway more than is absolutely necessary. Above all, we must avoid being brought back, like naughty children, by Nabuchodonosor. We take out our maps.[1] A good route has been chosen, which takes us from Bethlehem in a south-westerly direction past Hebron and Beersheba; we can, by keeping some miles west of the caravan road, avoid the hills of Idumæa on our left and the notice of

---

[1] For this chapter Sir George Adam Smith's excellent *Historical Atlas of The Holy Land* will be found useful. It will show, incidentally, that the pages which follow are not entirely dependent upon the imagination.

the Philistines on our right. There are water courses of
a kind, the merest *wadys* for the most part, which cut
across our path at intervals of thirty or forty miles.
Later on, when we get into the Wilderness of Shur,
there will be fewer desert streams and less opportunities of trapping game: the prospect is not encouraging.
While still in the land of Edom, with nothing but
limestone rocks to relieve the eye, we are always in
danger of being ambushed or rounded up like a herd of
cattle; when once the 'river of Egypt'[1] is crossed our
only danger will be one of starvation; we cannot have
it both ways.

When we began our journey there were barley fields
on every side. We have to admit—now that Juda's
barley fields are left behind for ever—that Nabuchodonosor has done his work well; only a few years
ago, and the same country was mostly desert, now it is
reclaimed and will bring prosperity to Palestine.
Looking back, in fact (from this uninteresting stage in
the journey—the southern Edom stage), we are
amazed at what the Babylonian monarch has managed
to do for Judea. It is always a mistake, of course, to
cast backward glances at either a land or a life which
one has decided to forget, but one cannot help noticing
that the country through which one has passed on the
early stages of this journey is a country well worth
stopping in. Yes, we are leaving what might have been
—had things gone on according to plan—a fruitful
return to husbandry. The crops which we saw by the
roadside: Chaldeans will benefit by them. The cattle
which we saw grazing on the hillside: Chaldeans will

[1] This is not, as its name suggests, the Nile, but a stream which
flows into the Mediterranean at least 150 miles east of the Nile.
The modern name for this river (which is not even a river all the year
round) is *Wady el Arish*.

feed their armies on them. The vines which we saw creeping up those endless lines of trellises: Chaldean wine-skins will be swelled by their juice. The orange and olive groves which gave us shelter in the midday heats, the fig-trees, the mango and apricot plantations: Chaldeans will enjoy all this.[1] Regrets are always idle, but one cannot help wondering whether perhaps it might not have been better to stop on, after all. Not only had nature and Nabuchodonosor been prepared to favour us as far as actual territory went, but with regard to politics and our position in the country we seem to have had equally powerful helps. Godolias (had he only been spared us) would have raised our fallen status; Jeremias (had he only been listened to) would have regained us the favour of the Lord. And both men would have continued to elicit the emperor's interest. Anyway, it is too late now, the map tells us that we are already well past Rehoboth.

.   .   .   .

We have managed, somehow, to cross the Wilderness of Shur. It is early morning, and we are hoping to make the first big town in Egypt before nightfall. The last ten days of travel have been a never-to-be-forgotten agony; the one sole consolation lay in the flatness of that frightful country. Bleak and featureless it may have been as scenery, but mercifully even from the point of view of wheels and horses' hoofs. Judea with its hills and villages and gardened estates is a thing of

---

[1] Not once but several times do we read of the remarkable success which was granted to the efforts of the post-destruction husbandmen in Judea. 'They gathered wine and a very great harvest' is almost a refrain; it is echoed in one form or another in the Prophecy from chapters xxxix to xliii. And it is interesting to notice that the history of this 'back to the land' movement is repeating itself to-day: Palestine is again becoming an agricultural country.

the past; it does not do to think of it. Our proper
concern is the present moment, and the present
moment has brought us to the border of Egypt.

From grey the skies are already turning to amber.
In a minute they will be changed to burning gold, and,
while the gentlest possible breeze is stirring in the palms,
the sun will rise triumphant over the horizon. Our
first day in the land of Egypt has begun.

.   .   .   .   .

Whatever the Egyptians are like as soldiers abroad
they are highly scientific as gardeners at home. The
Land of the Pharaohs, though naturally as dry as the
Land of the Prophets, is plentifully watered. The nearer
we approach the Delta of which we have heard so
much, the more often do we seem to be stepping over
a network of canals and streams. The country is as
flat as the Wilderness of Shur, but the yellowish sand
of the desert has given place—where the waterways
have not spread a carpet of green—to a dirty grey dust.
Grey, accordingly, are the mud-hut villages which
crouch in the sun and sleep. Now that we have left
Egypt's eastern boundary behind us, these villages
appear at closer intervals. They all seem to be exactly
alike: a few farms, a few fields, a yoke or two of honey-
coloured oxen pushing at a water-wheel or pulling at a
plough, an occasional goat, an occasional donkey, a
great number of children, and quantities upon quantities of flies. Between these clusters of habitation we
meet chains of camels, dreamy and superior, padding
flat-footed over the hot sand. Every now and then
our progress is delayed by a flock of sheep on its way
to some local market. The sheep of Egypt are fatter—
having less climbing to do—than those of Juda, and

bear the sign of some Egyptian god henna-stained across the rump.   In Egypt the fields seem to yield the same harvests as they do with us; [1] there are fewer vines and hardly any orange groves. What is wanting in the way of fruit familiar to our northern Juda is more than compensated for by the ubiquitous sugar-cane of the south. Sticks of this fibrous food are sucked by every native. [2]   Children hold it with both hands as they splash about at the water's edge: girls toy with it as they lean from windows gazing at the passers by; young men chew it as they drive along on mule-drawn carts to their work in the field or farm; old men pull at it between toothless gums as they sit in doorways gossiping. All whose hands are not otherwise occupied seem to be engaged in extracting the syrup from these pink and sticky rods.

.   .   .   .   .

It is almost noon. We dismount for the midday rest. Our shadows measure scarcely a foot's length on the burning road.   Our beasts, like our companions and ourselves, are streaming with sweat. We take what shelter we can in the shade of a cluster of fig-trees. How luxurious is the mere sight of green after the blinding glare of the Wilderness of Shur! At least in Egypt— even in the parts which are thinly populated—we

[1] It is still some centuries too early for the crops of rice and maize which will add to Egypt's prosperity later on. The 'Indian corn' which we see there to-day—unwrapping itself from its clumsy parcel of paper leaves—is an importation which seems to have followed the introduction of rice. Earlier than either of these is the cotton plant, which we see all over modern Egypt. It is not known when Egypt first became famous for cotton, but Pliny mentions Egyptian cotton in the second century A.D.

[2] Even the sugar cane was not originally an Egyptian product; it was brought from the east and used in Egypt for making a sweet-smelling incense as well as for purposes of eating. (See Jeremias vi, 20).

come upon these heaven-sent clumps of trees: fig, date,
eucalyptus and acacia. Gone for the most part is that
graceless swollen weed, the cactus, which was the only
form of plant hardy enough to brave the rigours of the
open desert. Never again do we wish to see that
monkey-puzzle of the east, the cactus; it may benefit
a lizard, but it is scant comfort to a man. We resume
our journey.

.   .   .   .   .

It is evening, and we are at the walls of Taphnis,
the *Tel Deffneh* of the Egyptians. The inhabitants of
the place come out and look at us. Two different
races, we take stock of each other. These men are
bigger and blacker than we. Not only in their size
and colour (burned darker, apparently, by an even
more merciless sun, and better conditioned, apparently,
on a diet of meat and cane), but also in their hair and
features, their teeth, their cheek-bones and their way of
standing, these southerners have little in common
with us of the Chosen Race. From the tinted whites
of their eyes to the pinks of their curved finger-nails
these men are of a different mould. Jeremias was right:
a more natural union would have been the union
between Juda and Babylon. But we have decided to
pledge ourselves to Egypt . . . and there is no going
back. In the twilight we are suddenly and sickeningly
conscious of our home-sickness. What is in store for
us among these full-lipped, wire-haired, flat-nosed
people who, wanton and yet apparently unconscious
of their nakedness, come out to stare at us in the
gathering gloom of dusk? We admit, O Lord, that we
are miserable, must we admit also that we have made a
mistake? 'O God of Israel, be our protection . . . O God
of Jacob, be our help.'

CHAPTER XIX

LAST PHASE

i

'A ND they came as far as Taphnis,' is the prophet's sole reference to the migration. One wishes he had told us who else from among the original Godolias household were on the journey. Baruch certainly, but what about the sons and brothers of the murdered man? Did the family follow the prophet's example, or did they go back to Masphath when the storm had blown over and try to eke out some sort of existence on the late governor's estate? Perhaps the reason why Jeremias does not answer these questions for us is because he feels that a unique chapter in Israel's chequered history has been closed for good. The rule of the commonwealth had never been tried before and was never to be tried again; the brief interlude was over.

At Taphnis, whether they wanted to settle there or not, the fugitive Jews would have had to wait. Though not on the border, Taphnis was the garrison town at which any who wanted to pass into the interior would have had to show their credentials; and an enormous horde of disreputable-looking aliens, travel-stained and unfamiliar with the language, must have had no very easy treatment at the hands of the Egyptian customs officials.

'And the word of the Lord came to Jeremias in Taphnis, saying: Take great stones in thy hand and hide them in the vault that is under the brick wall at the gate of Pharaoh's house in Taphnis, in the sight of all the men of Juda. And thou shalt say to them: Thus saith the Lord of hosts, the God of Israel: Behold I will send and take Nabuchodonosor the king of Babylon My servant, and I will set his throne over these stones which I have hid. And he shall come and strike the land of Egypt; such as are for death, for death; such as are for the sword, for the sword; such as are for captivity, for captivity.' (Then follows a long chapter which is believed to be the speech which accompanied the prophetical act; the closing words are to the effect that Pharaoh will be delivered into the hands of 'them that seek his life'.)

The reason why Jeremias was told to choose Taphnis for this symbolical enthronement of Nabuchodonosor—which we must examine more closely—is because that city would be the first to fall before the Chaldean invasion which his act prefigured. Memphis, Egypt's capital, was too far west to fall under the sudden hammer-blow of Babylon, and Rameses (which was nearer the border) had not at this time, apparently, the same political and military significance as Taphnis. Unfortunately there is no indication in the text as to how long Jeremias spent in the country of his exile before 'the word of the Lord came to him'. It is hardly likely that he was required to pronounce the fate of Pharaoh's house immediately on arrival. It is more probable that the defiant gesture was occasioned by infidelity on the part of the Jews after at least some months in Egypt. If we examine what the prophet said from the gate of Pharaoh's house, we see that it was not so much the sinfulness of Egypt, but the sinfulness of Israel, which drew from him the prophecy of Egypt's doom. One ventures to think, then, that the present episode came as a dramatic climax to a course of gradually increasing concessions on the part of the Jews towards the heathen practices of those with whom they were beginning to settle down. The Jews, as their fellows had been doing to a slightly less extent in Babylon at the other end of the continent, were adapting themselves only too well to the exile. Rightly had Jeremias cried out in the old days—as Isaias had cried out before him—that the Egyptians were no people with whom the Chosen Race should associate: they either let you down in battle or wore you down in faith. Thus the punishment which in the last-quoted extract is forecast as coming to the Pharaohs is chiefly to be understood in its effects upon the Hebrews. 'Destroy the hosts,' is the implication, 'and what will become of the guests?'

Since all military towns are, and presumably always have been, very much alike, we need waste no space in conjecturing a description of this one. Allowing for differences of fashion and racial custom, Taphnis would have had most points in common with its modern counterpart. You would have found the same barrack square, the same drinking shops, the same cabarets, the same songs, the same ladies of roomy principle, the same early morning marches through empty streets, the same manœuvres, the same trumpet-calls and the same sense of artificiality which you come across in any peace-time outpost of the empire. You get it all in Kipling and the works of P. C. Wren. So to turn straight to Jeremias.

'Take great stones and hide them in the vault,' was the Lord's instruction. Other versions than ours make the commission clearer to understand: 'mortar them into the brickwork of the forecourt' is a probable reading. The ceremony was intended to be a public one, and if it took place in a vault, it is difficult to see how 'all the people' could have followed what was going on. That the audience would have grasped the implications of the action—apart even from what Jeremias had to say about it—is undoubted: the laying of foundation-stones is a rite which is immemorial. The fact that a foundation-stone was being laid when the building had been founded long before would have had but one possible explanation. The palace which stood massive before the eyes of the assembled crowd was but a makeshift thing—at best a house prepared for a future occupant. The audacity of the act is staggering. On the very steps of Pharaoh's garrison palace a foreigner prophet was preparing for a dynasty which was to oust the occupant of Pharaoh's throne.

If it were not for the fierceness which is breathed by this section of the Prophecy we would be tempted to postulate of the watching crowd a great shout of joy. Jeremias, standing there in the sun, with his trowel in one hand and a mason's hod in the other, must have been a brave sight. But when we read his long speech we realise that there was no answering enthusiasm from his audience. As at his previous discourse to the same people in Chamaam near Bethlehem,

Jeremias grew more and more stern as the flood of his
oratory was loosed upon his hearers. This sternness
was due, surely, to the expression which he saw upon
the face of the crowd—the expression of sullen disapproval. How well he had come to know that look!
But Jeremias, still the splendid rebel, could defy the
people of Israel as he had defied the policies of Israel's
kings. He could defy the people of Israel as he was
even now defying the power of Egypt.

Seeing that he was defying the power of Egypt, it is
perhaps astonishing that he was not arrested. Aliens
are seldom at liberty to tamper with property belonging to the Crown, and Jeremias had spent quite half an
hour mixing his mortar, adjusting his tablet, smoothing
off his handiwork and addressing his fellow exiles.
Why did not the Taphnis authorities interfere? A few
possible reasons suggest themselves. In the first place
the Egyptians are an indolent people, and one can well
imagine that a Taphnis official would have taken longer
than, say, a Babylonian or a Syrian or Medish official
to realise what was going on. Again, the ceremony
was being conducted in a language which was but
imperfectly, if at all, understood. Also the central
figure was doing something which was so obviously
resented by the people for whom he was doing it that
there could be no danger of a Jewish rising. If inter-
ference were necessary at all it might have to be in
defence of the prophet and not in his suppression. Thus,
to venture a tentative reconstruction, I picture the
following:

From one of unsympathetic silence the attitude of
the crowd in the forecourt changes to one of murmuring hostility. The people of Egypt, uninterested in

the doings of the refugees, take no very great account of the matter at first. They watch from the comparative cool of their doorways as they would have watched a dog-fight or an itinerant magician. They see that someone is doing something to the pavement in front of the main gate, but since the precise nature of the operation is screened from view, and since the Jews have proved a law-abiding lot since their arrival a year ago, and since they have probably got permission to do whatever they are doing, and since it is the business of the palace guard to see to these things, and since the king is not likely to be back in Taphnis for at least six months . . . what is the use of doing anything about it?[1]

As to how the meeting finally closed there is nothing to give us the slightest clue. One imagines that from murmuring hostility the emotion of the crowd swelled to active hostility, and that stones were seized and thrown at the thundering prophet. Jeremias had met this sort of thing before; it would not have disturbed him greatly. That the prophet escaped with his life on this occasion is, from negative evidence, almost certain. Tradition reserves for Jeremias at least three possible deaths, not one of which is placed at the climax of to-day's discourse. But with legend's vagaries we must deal in a final chapter.

.   .   .   .   .

Taphnis is closing down for the night. The palace

[1] Since Memphis was the capital, it is unlikely that the kings of Egypt would spend more than a third of the year in the winter residence at Taphnis. Ruins of this garrison palace, incidentally, have been found on the site of what was once Taphnis, and it is Sir Flinders Petrie's claim that part of the pavement into which Jeremias built his tablet still exists.

steps are littered with bits of peel, scraps of food, leaves of unrecognisable vegetables, crushed and twisted sticks of the inevitable sugar-cane, offal—refuse, in fact, of every kind and smell. Below, in the open square, lizards and grasshoppers flick their nervous way over the black surface of dust. Frogs croak their evening salutations to each other in the muddy banks of the canal which regularly once a year keeps Taphnis from dying of thirst. Somewhere in the fields a boy is picking out a tune on a reed. Over and over again the plaintive melody is repeated. The wail of his cadences is carried over the water, and the man who is crouching knee-deep in the warm slime among the rushes uses the refrain on which to rest the repetition of his prayer. When the last frog has ceased its throaty song and when the last light has been snuffed out in the line of huts that flank the water's edge, a prophet of Israel (aged between sixty and seventy) comes out from his hiding-place and scrapes the mud from his legs with a handful of weeds. He stands on the bank for a moment as if bracing himself to meet a demand, and then turns and walks silently along the road to Memphis . . . or to Magdal, or to Rameses, or to On—to anywhere where there may still be colonies of Jews. In Taphnis, for the time being, he can be no further use.

But as for us (we, that is, who have stopped out of doors from curiosity, and who are now walking back in the moonlight to our lodgings beyond the palace), we have heard the prophet's voice for the last time. If Jeremias is to preach again—as he surely must—the echo of his words will never come our way; the only witness to Jeremias's last sermon is the consequence which tradition has attributed to his words. I mean his death.

ii

A section to do with the vindication of Jeremias's Taphnis prophecy seems called for. I append accordingly the conclusions of scholars. 'Putting together two cuneiform records and a hieroglyphic inscription, it appears that in his thirty-seventh year Nebuchadrezzer penetrated as far as Syene. There he was met and repulsed by Egyptian troops. Two years later the Babylonians renewed the invasion, and by their complete success forced Egypt to pay tribute.' This is a quotation from Dr Cheyne's *Jeremiah* (page 197). Professor Lods gives the date of this Babylonian triumph as 568 B.C. Driver likewise accepts the evidence, and is supported (if I read him aright) by the more recent authority on Jeremias, L. E. Binns.[1] Thus it is abudantly clear that as far as Babylon's invasion of Egypt went, Jeremias was proved correct in his predictions. But there were two other points, consequences of the predicted invasion, which were forecast in the Taphnis sermon—namely, Pharaoh's overthrow and the deliverance of the exiled Jews into Babylonian hands for captivity or the sword. How far were these prophecies fulfilled? With regard to Pharaoh Hophra we have no very certain information beyond the facts already given. This much, however, might be added: Hophra was, according to Herodotus (who calls him Apries), already beginning to lose the con-

[1] In *The Book of The Prophet Jeremiah*, p. 308, where the writer quotes at the same time W. M. Muller's doubt about the Chaldean inscriptions in question. The material for arriving at a decision is, as Mr. Binns says, very slight. The same author gives further grounds for believing that his 'not improbable' subjection of Egypt to Babylon took place between the years of 569-525 B.C.

fidence of his people some six or seven years before the
end of his reign. It appears that the Egyptian losses
against the Cyreneans were put down to Hophra's
faulty generalship, so that by the year 568 the king
fell an easy victim to his enemies. It is not quite clear
whether it was Nabuchodonosor or Hophra's successor, Amasis, who was responsible for bringing the
reign to an end. Herodotus obtained his information
from the priests of Egypt, and so the part played by
Nabuchodonosor is naturally kept in the background.
We can note, incidentally, that in the prophecy about
Pharaoh's overthrow Jeremias does not say which
Pharaoh it is that Nabuchodonosor will oust from the
throne, nor does he say—if we take it that he must
have meant the reigning sovereign—that Hophra's
Babylonian enemies would put him to death; Jeremias
may quite well have had in mind Hophra's nearer
enemies, the dissatisfied members of the Egyptian
court. This last point should be borne in mind if we
read on in our Herodotus and come across the reference to Hophra's death, nine years after his dethrone-
ment, at the hands of Amasis. Incidentally, Hophra
appears to have been strangled.

The third and last prediction which needs to be looked
at in its verification is the threat against the Jewish
exiles themselves. Jeremias says that 'yet a small
number' shall escape both the sword and the captivity.
That by far the greater number perished by the sword
and in captivity may be assumed from the fact that
they shared the same fortunes as the Egyptians with
whom they had only too successfully identified themselves. If Egypt was hard hit, then so were they. But
even if we are unwilling to make this assumption we

may take Jeremias's words in another sense, and say that, owing to their rejection of the Lord, the Jews in Egypt would *as Jews* be very nearly exterminated. Juda would forfeit her right to call herself God's People. That a small body of faithful Jews survived both the ravages of war and the contamination of unbelief is certain. We know that whenever Jewish colonists came to Egypt in subsequent generations Hebrew practices were not unknown. In fact, it may have been the knowledge that Hebrew centres existed in Egypt that attracted the various groups of future settlers. Josephus, the Jewish historian, tells how Ptolemy Lagi (Alexander the Great's successor) sent quantities of Jews into Egypt. From that time onwards the Jews assumed considerable political and financial importance in Egypt. Their religion waned, but their prestige waxed; so that by the date of the Holy Family's flight into Egypt a secularised Judaism would have been found spread throughout the land. 'I will punish them that dwell in the land of Egypt as I have punished Jerusalem,' had been the words of the Lord to Jeremias. Mary and Joseph, entering Egypt with the Infant Christ, would have seen a strange vindication of the threat. Not with poverty had the Jewish colonies been punished, but with prosperity. The men of Juda had fallen under a more grievous curse than that of famine, they were cursed with the evil of finance.

CHAPTER XX

CONCLUSION

i

HAVING followed Jeremias through fifty years of ministry and forty-three chapters of prophecy, we come now to the work of filling in and summing up: we fill in with the assistance of tradition, and sum up on the evidence of the Prophecy itself. Let us do the summing up first; it can be done more shortly than the other.

If history has dealt hardly with Jeremias, it is on two heads only: his indifference to the Jewish sense of patriotism and his lack of a lighter side. Our Lord is charged with the same defects. But why should prophets be raised up by God to tell us to do what instinctively we do already? If a prophet has a certain definite message to deliver he will not waste time insisting on the necessity of national spirit and a sense of humour. Jeremias, rather than compromise on things which he held to be essential, has given to mankind an exterior which suggests rigidity. So has the Church. The truth is that, in surrendering to the essentials all that was accidental, Jeremias surrendered to the ideal of human nature all that was trivial in human intercourse. And people who do this are liable to be misunderstood. The world sees only the surface, and is able to understand the superficial. The deep things very often escape it altogether. There was no

one less superficial than Jeremias. But if others failed
to understand Jeremias, he on his part understood
others. 'Having known misery,' Virgil makes Dido
say to Æneas, 'I have learned to pity the miserable.'
Which is why Jeremias went into voluntary exile with
his people.

Of the man's life and labour, then, it might be said
that, nerved in an unusually high degree to appreciate
both his people's need and his own inability to meet
that need, and at the same time refusing to be blinded
by the discouragement which he felt, Jeremias continued all his life to speak, to suffer and to give,
until the very issues which he served were withdrawn
from the field of his endeavour. Sensitive, loving,
and—for all his many chapters—unable fully to express
himself, the prophet was forced to be the helpless
witness of his country's shame. Struggle though he
might to obtain it, the final yielding to Babylon was
mourned by none more deeply than by him. Indeed,
it was the way in which Juda met this scourge that
spelled for Jeremias alike the downfall of the people
he loved and the failure of which he himself felt
guilty. To Jeremias can the words be applied, that
'being approved by the testimony of faith, he received
not the promise, God providing some better thing for
his reward'.[1] Though feeling the hand of God heavy
upon his shoulders, Jeremias is scarcely to be pitied.
They that sow in tears shall reap in joy.[2]

Or we can again quote the words which provided us
with a text at the start: 'struggle, man against men,
defiance . . . the essence of all drama . . . a splendid
rebel.'

[1] Hebrews xi, 39, 40.   [2] Psalm cxxv, 5.

ii

To turn now from the task of summing up to that of filling in, we have first to account for those chapters which come after that point in the text where the prophet's activities cease.   Most of the remaining prophecies (as the synopsis in the Appendix shows) are repetitions of earlier events or sermons.   The forty-fifth chapter is a curious little five-versed insertion belonging to Joachim's reign and telling Baruch not to make mountains out of mole-hills.   In the encouragement given to the downcast Baruch a prophecy is included which spares him from a death by violence: 'I will give thee thy life and save thee,' says the Lord.   Whatever is in store for the master as a result of his ministry, at least the secretary can rest secure. 'And dost thou seek for thyself great things?'— this is the reproof referred to when Baruch first came into the story—'Seek not.'   Abrupt, straightforward, bearing no grudge, perfect from the literary point of view, entirely suitable. A snub? The brave and faithful Baruch is built to take it.

From the forty-sixth to the fifty-first chapter the text amounts simply to a series of prophecies attacking various nations.   That Babylon shares the censures of Egypt, Philistia, Tyre, Moab and the rest is ample indication that Jeremias was not suffered to deceive himself in his pro-Chaldean bias.   The last chapter, the fifty-second, is a recapitulation of Sedecias's reign, together with a statement of the material consequences which Nabuchodonosor's taking of Jerusalem involved. And that is all.   But before we allow the prophet to slip out of this book as he has slipped out of his Prophecy we must catch at one or two of the legends which shroud his wasted frame, and see whether they do not add more than is commonly added by legend to the lives of famous men. We get no information from Baruch regarding Jeremias's death. Nor do Egyptian or Babylonian records help us. We have to make what we can of father-to-son traditions.

iii

Of the three main lines of conjecture regarding the prophet's closing years and death there is the theory (to take the least satisfactory one first) that he was taken away by Nabuchodonosor when Babylon finally subdued Egypt. This makes Jeremias die in the Chaldean capital. It is certainly not an impossible theory, but it does not seem a very probable one. The developed version of this view, which has it that Jeremias lived on in Babylon to see the release of Joachin from prison in the reign of Evil-Merodach, brings the prophet to a very great age indeed. He would have been a good eighty-five at the time of Joachin's release, and it is not even claimed that he died immediately afterwards. The average age of man was then, apparently, considerably shorter than it is now.

One objection which might reasonably be raised against this theory is, that had Jeremias spent all those years at Nabuchodonosor's court, then surely Daniel, who was a member of the same court, would have mentioned him. Again, why should Nabuchodonosor consult the very junior prophet, Daniel, if the senior prophet and his friend of twenty years' standing were available. But apart from this kind of objection there is another kind of objection which usually carries far more weight. It is that we find ourselves shrinking from the idea of a Jeremias who has always been so independent, so fight-to-the-finish, so speak-out-to-kings-and-princes, now ending his life as a salaried companion to an alien king. If a foreign capital must be the scene of the prophet's death, we would rather it were Memphis than Babylon—in penury rather than in plenty. If Jeremias must be yoked to an alien sovereign, then let it be to Hophra rather than to Nabuchodonosor—resisting rather than responding. All his life Jeremias has been a reactionary, and to let him die without a challenge on his lips is, we feel, to rob him of something of his unity. Such a course of argument has obviously no validity whatever; it is only that we like to think, when reading St John's account of the Last Supper, that Our Lord had Jeremias in mind as He spoke of the persecutions which are the privilege of the apostolate.

iv

The second tradition which comes up for examination is the one which makes Jeremias come back from Egypt to die in Jerusalem. There exists to-day a hermit's cave or grotto outside the northern wall of Jerusalem; it is appropriately situated on the hill of Golgotha and overlooks the Holy City in the direction of Herod's gate. Since at least the fourteenth century this spot has been identified with the burial-place of Jeremias.[1] The grotto was certainly there in Jeremias's

[1] There is a short description of it in Thomson, *The Land and The Book*, p. 368, Cheyne, op. cit. p. 179, and other works; picture post cards of Jeremias's Grotto are on sale everywhere in Jerusalem.

time, and there is nothing to say that he did not live in it. One very much doubts, however, if he died in it. A more likely theory as regards the tenancy of the cave would be the view that he occupied it at intervals during the years 621-587 and 586-583. These dates represent those times, from the finding of Deuteronomy onwards, when Jeremias was not either in prison or in Egypt. It may have been during these unidentified periods of retreat that Jeremias wrote the Book of Lamentations. Certainly he could not have had a better setting for the work. We can picture him sitting in the mouth of his rocky cave and gazing out towards the irresponsive city; here, with sun-bleached skulls all round him and carrion circling over his head and scorpions creeping about in the sand at his feet, would have been an ideal place in which to write a book like Lamentations. Unfortunately it is this picture which has survived when all the other pictures have perished. [1] It is not claimed here that such a picture is a false one— in fact I have just been saying that it is probably a true one—we merely claim that it is not the most truly characteristic. But whether or not Jeremias ever occupied the grotto which bears his name and whether —if he did—he wrote Lamentations there, certain it is that the tradition which connects the prophet's death-bed with the site is not one to find great favour. And if you ask why not, it can only be said (as was said in the foregoing section) that to end the prophet thus does not seem true to the whole. That the ruins of Jerusalem, moss-grown and rat-ridden and desolate,

---

[1] See Cheyne, op. cit. p. 179, who gives us this melancholy memory of Jeremias, and is supported in the pictures given by Binns, Williams, Stanley, etc. (See Binns, Introduction, op. cit. pp. xxxix-xliii.)

were towards the close of his life haunted by the aged
man of action, who, seated on a broken column like
some pale Victorian ghost or sheltering in the shadow
of a crumbling Temple arch, wrote his sombre testament, is altogether out of keeping. But this is admit-
tedly no argument.

v

The last and in every way the most probable tradition has it that Jeremias was stoned to death in Egypt
by the Jews. The scene is commonly given as Taphnis
(so the Roman Martyrology for example), but the date
is not so much as conjectured. It almost certainly took
place—allowing that the first part of the tradition
is correct—before Nabuchodonosor's invasion and
Hophra's deposition. 'Saint Jeremias, Prophet and
Martyr': this is surely the most satisfactory finish to
the story. And if the title of martyr is not vouched for
according to the requirements of historical research,
at least the other two titles are justified beyond dispute.

May I tender my own, unsupported, reconstruction
of the prophet's last hours on earth? It is as follows.

Jeremias has been preaching for some months up
and down the Delta provinces. Word has reached him
that Baruch, whom he has left behind in Taphnis to
look after what is still the largest body of Jews in
Egypt, is dying. He has hurried back to Taphnis,
only to find on arrival that his friend has been dead for
some days.[1] If Jeremias is too late to see his friend

---

[1] Unless Baruch did, as a fact, die before his master, it is difficult
to account for the fact that there is no mention of Jeremias's death
in any of the works which were written by Baruch.

alive he is not too late to pray beside him at his grave. And so the prophet, deciding to visit the place of burial, walks along the banks of the canal towards the Jewish quarter of the town. He has been travelling all night and he is sad. He is wondering about the manner of Baruch's death; not that he suspects a death by violence—he knows well enough that the Lord has not gone back upon His promise—but he wonders whether his friend died alone or whether any of his fellow Jews remained at his side to pray . . . he wonders whether the proper rites were carried out, whether the body was wrapped in linen cloths and anointed with oils and spices 'as the manner of the Jews is to bury'. Knowing the Jews and their weariness of the old religion, he doubts it.

In passing Pharaoh's palace, Jeremias is met by a great concourse of people moving across the open square. The prophet halts for a moment and remembers that to-day is one of Egypt's religious festivals. The man of God becomes the unwilling spectator of a heathen rite. The procession bars his way. Since by this time it is too late to go back, Jeremias, with his shoulder-blades pressing against a wall and with the intention of keeping as far out of sight as possible, prepares to make the best of it. Occupied with his thoughts about Baruch, and paying perhaps little attention at first to what is going on around him, the prophet suddenly recognises a familiar face in the procession . . . then another . . . and another . . .

The Chosen People have sold their birthright once again: the sons of Israel are paying homage to the gods of Egypt.

Sick with misery, Jeremias closes his eyes. But what

he has seen refuses to be blotted out. So, after all his work, it has come to this! He washes his hands of the whole thing. *Nunc dimittis servum Tuum Domine*, for Thy servant can do no more.

And then, leaning giddy against his wall, Jeremias wonders whether perhaps there *is* not something more he can do. The thought grows, and he finds himself shrinking from its consequences. All the old fears, all the old loathings, all the old desires for escape come back to him. In a split instant of time he is back again at the beginning of his prophetical life, he is hearing the summons over again . . . and he is making the same replies. 'Ah, ah, ah, Lord God,' he cries in his agony, 'behold, I cannot speak, for I am—not now a child any longer, but an equally useless old man—a broken, unsuccessful, dispirited old man with no generosity left.' But even while he is framing his refusals he knows that he has as good as yielded to the Lord. *For thou shalt go to all that I shall send thee*, he hears again after all these years; *be not afraid at their presence, for I am with thee, saith the Lord*. The command has been repeated.

How old did we say he was? Seventy? Seventy-five? It doesn't matter, it is not too late.

Jeremias is forcing his way through the crowd, pressing as well as he can up the palace steps, climbing on to the raised parapet from which he has spoken to the people of Taphnis once before. Raised above the mob, Jeremias stands gasping for breath, throws up his arms in a wild gesture of arrest, and begins. 'Return, beloved of the Lord, to Him Who has called you out of darkness. Go not after your own devices . . . ' A stone flies past the prophet's head and falls bounding and

ringing on the marble pavement of Pharaoh Hophra's
court.

It is thus—crystallised or, as it were, photographed
—that I have my last vision of Jeremias the prophet.
It shows me an old man looking down from a height
upon hundreds of men and women who are massed in
the square in front of him. Though I see only their
backs I know that these people are Jews and not
Egyptians. The prophet's bare arms, black against the
sky, are rigid above his head. The head itself, fringed
with an irregular halo of grey wispish hair, is held high
and is supported by a gaunt rope-like throat. The eyes
are wide open, but not, I think, in anger or even in
reproach.

As I look at this picture of my mind I smell the hot
bodies and hear the roar of Jewish hate. Though the
prophet's lips are parted I can catch nothing of his
message. But ringing through the voice of the crowd
I hear another Voice—deathless and not to be silenced
by mortal man—echoing down the centuries . . . 'Jerusalem, Jerusalem, that killest the prophets and stonest
them that are sent to thee, how often would I have
gathered thy children as the bird doth her brood under
her wings . . . and thou wouldst not?'[1]

And by the side of my vision of Jeremias—out of the
corner of my eye (forgive me if I am being tedious)—
I see another. It is a picture which reveals the massive
form of an elderly Ethiopian who is pressing against
an Egyptian mob. Abdemelech, tears streaming down
his ebony cheeks, is trying desperately to keep his
people from a hideous crime.

[1] Luke xiii, 34.

APPENDIX A

A Rough Synopsis of the Prophecy

(i) Delivered between 627 B.C. and 608 B.C.

CHAPTERS

i	The Call.
ii-iv	Early Sermons.
v-vi	The Scythian Question.
vii-x	Idolatry and Impenitence.
xi-xiii	Deuteronomy.
xiv-xvii	General Sermons.

(ii) Delivered between 608 B.C. and 597 B.C.

CHAPTERS

xviii, xix	Pottery Sermons.
xx, xxvi	Jeremias in the Stocks.
xxii-xxv	General Sermons.

(iii) Delivered after 597 B.C.

CHAPTERS

xxvii-xxix	Against False Prophecy.
xxx-xxxix	The Restoration.
xl-xlv	An Appendix giving Subsequent History.
xlvi-li	Against Egypt and Other Nations.
lii	Summing up of Sedecias's Reign.

APPENDIX B

WHAT is printed below is simply the combined texts of chapters twenty and twenty-six so arranged as to form what I conceive to be a single event. With Jeremias's later chapter in italics the passage reads:

'*The priests and the prophets and all the people laid hold on him, saying: Let him be put to death. And all the people were gathered together against Jeremias in the house of the Lord.* And Phassur struck Jeremias the prophet, and put him in the stocks that were in the upper gate of Benjamin, in the house of the Lord. *And the princes of Juda heard these words, and they went up from the king's house into the house of the Lord and sat in the entry of the new gate of the house of the Lord. And the priests and the prophets spoke to the princes and the people, saying: The judgement of death is for this man because he hath prophesied against this city as you have heard with your ears.* And when it was light the next day Phassur brought Jeremias out of the stocks. And Jeremias said to him: The Lord hath not called thy name Phassur, but Fear on Every Side . . . thou and all thy house shall go into captivity and there thou shalt die . . . thou and all thy friends.' (Here Jeremias, realising that he is about to die, turns to the Lord) 'Thou hast deceived me, O Lord, and I am deceived . . . for I am speaking now this long time crying out against iniquity and often proclaiming devastation. And the word of the Lord is made a reproach to me, and a derision all the day . . *Then Jeremias spoke to all the princes and to all the people, saying: The Lord is with me to prophesy concerning this house and concerning this city all the words that you have heard. Now therefore amend your ways and your doings, and hearken to the voice of the Lord your God . . . but as for me, behold I am in your hands: do with me what is good and right in your eyes.'* (And then aside to the Lord in prayer) 'And Thou, O Lord of hosts, prover of the just, Who seest the reins and the heart, let me see, I beseech Thee, Thy vengeance upon them, for to Thee have I laid open my cause. *Then the princes and all the people said to the priests and to the prophets: There is no judgment of death for this man.* Then Jeremias said: Sing ye to the Lord, praise ye the Lord, because He hath delivered the soul of the poor out of the hand of the wicked.'

BIBLIOGRAPHY

Batten, Loring W., *The Hebrew Prophet*, 1905.

Binns, *The Book of the Prophet Jeremiah*, 1919.

Barnes, *Chronicles (Cambridge Bible Series)*, 1899.

Cheyne, *Jeremiah, His Life and Times*, 1888.

Driver, *Deuteronomy (International Critical Commentary)*, 1895.

Driver, *The Book of The Prophet Jeremiah*, 1906.

Gore, Goudge, Guillaume, *New Commentary on Holy Scripture*, 1928.

Hastings, *Dictionary of the Bible*, 1899.

Lods, *The Prophets and The Rise of Judaism*, 1937.

Meistermann, *Guide to The Holy Land*, 1923.

Moran, *Introduction to Scripture*, 1937.

Old Testament, The, (Cambridge Summer School Lectures), 1938.

Peake, *Commentary on The Bible*, 1924.

Pinches, *The Old Testament in The Light of Historical Records*, 1903.

Pope, *'Aids' to The Bible, Vol. 2, O.T.*, 1930.

Rawson Lumby, *The Second Book of Kings*, 1892.

Smith, Sir G. A., *Historical Atlas of The Holy Land*, 1937.[1]

Smith, W., *Dictionary of The Bible*.

Streane, *Jeremiah and Lamentations*, 1892.

Thomson, *The Land and The Book*, 1876.

Also appropriate articles in *The Catholic Encyclopædia, The Encyclopædia Britannica* and *The Story of The Bible*.

---

[1] Though of an unwieldy size, these maps are invaluable for any serious study of the Bible; even to the amateur student they can be of absorbing interest. The Chronological Tables alone, apart altogether from the plates, repay the closest examination.